NIGHT

IN THE SAME SERIES:

WHERE THE SILENCE RINGS
A Literary Companion to Mountains

DARK WATERS DANCING TO A BREEZE
A Literary Companion to Rivers & Lakes

DESERTS
A Literary Companion

GARDENS
A Literary Companion

THE SEA
A Literary Companion

SERIES EDITOR: WAYNE GRADY

edited and with an introduction by
MERILYN SIMONDS

NIGHT

A LITERARY COMPANION

 David Suzuki Foundation

 GREYSTONE BOOKS
D&M PUBLISHERS INC.
Vancouver / Toronto / Berkeley

09 10 11 12 13   5 4 3 2 1

Greystone Books
A division of D&M Publishers Inc.
2323 Quebec Street, Suite 201
Vancouver BC Canada V5T 4S7
www.greystonebooks.com

David Suzuki Foundation
219–2211 West 4th Avenue
Vancouver BC Canada V6K 4S2

Library and Archives Canada Cataloguing in Publication
Night : a literary companion / edited by Merilyn Simonds.

ISBN 978-1-55365-396-7

1. Night—Literary collections.   1. Simonds, Merilyn, 1949–

PN6071.N5N54 2009   820.8′033   C2008-907683-4

Jacket and text design by Peter Cocking
Typeset by Naomi MacDougall
Jacket image from Mary Evans Picture Library
Printed and bound in Canada by Friesens
Printed on acid-free paper that is forest friendly (100% post-consumer recycled paper)
and has been processed chlorine free.
Distributed in the U.S. by Publishers Group West

We gratefully acknowledge the financial support of the Canada Council for the Arts,
the British Columbia Arts Council, the Province of British Columbia through the Book
Publishing Tax Credit, and the Government of Canada through the Book Publishing
Industry Development Program (BPIDP) for our publishing activities.

CONTENTS

INTRODUCTION

———

WHEN I WAS a girl, I couldn't wait for night to fall. Darkness was delicious. It was a time for games of mystery and masquerade: hide-and-seek, statues, murder in the dark. The landscape moved in close, shapes shifted to silver, the air thickened with night scents, birds stopped their singing, and in the stillness, I heard my own heart. Years passed, and the night became a time for linked fingers and soft kisses. I looked up and saw the stars. Now I watch the full moon rising, wondering if the tomatoes need blanketing against frost. I tilt my head on a mid-August night and see the star-stones drop to Earth.

When it comes to the night, language is imprecise. Night doesn't fall; not really. It rises, coming first to the indents in the landscape, the valleys and coulees, the notch below our house where a thin stream flows. Slowly, it ascends the riverbank, the hillsides, moving east to west, until all is darkness except the gold-tipped trees and a pale ruddy smear where the sun once was. Each cycle of light and dark is called a day—weeks and months are calculated as accumulations of days—yet night could just as easily be the measure. A year is 365 nights long, too. But it is not the night so much as the slide into darkness that arouses our linguistic imagination: sundown, twilight, dusk, the gloaming, evensong, vespers, crepuscule, blindman's holiday, cockshut, owl-let, star-rush.

Historically, night was a time of shutting in, closing down. The night air was considered pestilent, malignant. Evil lurked. There is something atavistic about this terror of the night, a throwback to a time when predators, asleep by day, prowled the darkness. By the late 1600s, John Locke was philosophizing that the almost universal childhood fear of the dark came from nannies telling ghost stories to wide-eyed youngsters. Almost a century later, Edmund Burke came closer to the truth. Darkness, he wrote in *A Philosophical Enquiry into the Origin of Our Ideas of the Sublime and Beautiful* (1757) is "terrible in its own nature."

But there are other points of view. In *This Cold Heaven* (2001), Gretel Ehrlich recounts a Greenland myth in which the world exists in a darkness that admits no death. Before long, there are too many people. Two crones discuss the problem. One says, "Let us do without daylight if at the same time we can be without death," but the other insists, "Nay . . . we will have both Light and Death." This is an odd anomaly in a world where the darkness of night is equated with the absence of life— physical, intellectual, spiritual. The supposed retreat from civilization in the first millennium was called the Dark Ages. When

Jane Jacobs wrote about the bleak future, she called her book *Dark Age Ahead* (2004).

Our fear of the dark, or at least the aspersions we cast on it, may be rooted in poor eyesight. As Wayne Grady points out in his essay "Nocturne" (2006), excerpted here, "We haven't always been that way; far back in the evolutionary history of our species, we were nocturnal creatures. When we emerged from the night, we traded in night vision for color vision, and darkness has frightened us ever since." As if to compensate for our stunted vision, other senses bloom at night. Sounds, in particular, are exaggerated. The mice that race across my bedroom ceiling sound like foxes; the howling coyote could be Cerberus himself. It is true what the Italians say: In the night, every cat is a leopard.

Before artificial illumination, those who wandered about at night were liable to trip over tree roots or fall headlong into open wells. In the city, as William Hogarth's marvelous engraving *Night* (1738) attests, midnight strollers were at the mercy of broken pavement, wayward coaches, and showers of "night waste" from the rooms above. The French proverb still holds: Good people love the day; bad people, the night. Theft, arson, and more horrendous crimes take place under the cover of darkness, as Elie Wiesel makes clear in *Night* (1960), a memoir of his nighttime arrival at the glowing chimneys of Auschwitz. At one time, soldiers waited until dawn to attack, but in the age of guerrilla warfare, as Tim O'Brien points out in "Night Life" (1990), battles are fought hand to hand in the dark.

Isaac Asimov, in his classic science fiction story "Night-fall" (1941), posited a world perpetually illuminated by six suns. Once every two thousand years, a massive eclipse plunged the planet into a darkness that drove the populace mad. It's not inconceivable. Even the momentary disappearance of our solitary sun is cause for unsettled wonder, as Annie Dillard illustrates in "Total Eclipse" (1982).

So great is our distrust of night that we've devised an electric six-sun equivalent that turns night bright as day, stripping it of superstition and silence, inhabiting it with both work and play. Of course, we've always worked at night. "Nightmen" emptied the cesspools after dark, which was when the grave diggers (and grave robbers) were out, especially during plagues. And the seasons have never been a respecter of sleep: when the time is ripe for sowing and harvesting, the fields beckon, just as the barn does when the ewe begins to lamb. I remember a summer night when we first moved to the country; I awoke to a low roar in the distance. Shafts of light swept the bedroom walls like intermittent searchlights. Aliens, I thought; but no, it was the farmer across the road, on his combine at midnight, hell-bent on bringing in the corn before the autumn rains fell.

Illuminating the night was never a universally popular move. In the early 1800s, Pope Gregory XVI forbade streetlamps in Rome, arguing that the citizenry would gather at night to foment rebellion. Artificial light was considered an interference in the divine plan for the world, which ordained darkness as much as light. Because the streets of the rich were lit first, outdoor lighting became a symbol of class and privilege: the streetlamps were the first to go after the storming of the Bastille. And now, again, the lighting of the night is in disfavor—a disruption to migrating birds, a drain on resources, a blight—as Timothy Ferris points out in "Beginnings" (2002), on the feral beauty of a deeply dark sky.

The stars, the moon, the whip-poor-will, fireflies, bats, and skunks: these essays introduce the peculiar landscape and inhabitants, the shape and smell and shadowy significance of that constant companion to human lives, the night.

Merilyn Simonds

THE RAVEN
STEALS THE LIGHT

———

BILL REID AND ROBERT BRINGHURST

Creation myths the world over, from the Mayan Popul Vuh to the Christian Bible, cite darkness as the murky oblivion from which life arose. Nyx, the Greek goddess of night, spawned a brood of dark spirits including Sleep, Death, Strife, Pain, and the three Fates. By contrast, the Hindu goddess of night, Ratri, is an uncharacteristically benevolent deity who is invoked for protection against robbers and wolves. Most often it is light, whether from God, or Prometheus, or Raven, that is the mythologically precious gift. This Haida tale comes from Canada's Pacific Northwest Coast and is retold by acclaimed poet Robert Bringhurst (1946–) and renowned artist Bill Reid (1920–1998). In it, Raven tricks an old hoarder into releasing the light that becomes the sun, the stars, and the moon.

· · ·

BEFORE THERE WAS anything, before the great flood had covered the earth and receded, before the animals walked the earth or the trees covered the land or the birds flew between the trees, even before the fish and the whales and seals swam in the sea, an old man lived in a house on the bank of a river with his only child, a daughter. Whether she was as beautiful as hemlock fronds against the spring sky at sunrise or as ugly as a sea slug doesn't really matter very much to this story, which takes place mainly in the dark.

Because at that time the whole world was dark. Inky, pitchy, all-consuming dark, blacker than a thousand stormy winter midnights, blacker than anything anywhere has been since.

The reason for all this blackness has to do with the old man in the house by the river, who had a box which contained a box which contained a box which contained an infinite number of boxes each nestled in a box slightly larger than itself until finally there was a box so small all it could contain was all the light in the universe.

The Raven, who of course existed at that time, because he had always existed and always would, was somewhat less than satisfied with this state of affairs, since it led to an awful lot of blundering around and bumping into things. It slowed him down a good deal in his pursuit of food and other fleshly pleasures, and in his constant effort to interfere and to change things.

Eventually, his bumbling around in the dark took him close to the home of the old man. He first heard a little singsong voice muttering away. When he followed the voice, he soon came to the wall of the house, and there, placing his ear against the planking, he could just make out the words, "I have a box and inside the box is another box and inside it are many more boxes, and in the smallest box of all is all the light in the world, and it is mine and I'll never give any of it to anyone, not even my daughter, because, who knows, she may be as homely as a sea slug, and neither she nor I would like to know that."

It took only an instant for the Raven to decide to steal the light for himself, but it took a lot longer for him to invent a way to do so.

First he had to find a door into the house. But no matter how many times he circled it or how carefully he felt the planking, it remained a smooth, unbroken barrier. Sometimes he heard either the old man or his daughter leave the house to get water or for some other reason, but they always departed from the side of the house opposite to him, and when he ran around to the other side the wall seemed as unbroken as ever.

Finally the Raven retired a little way upstream and thought and thought about how he could enter the house. As he did so, he began to think more and more of the young girl who lived there, and thinking of her began to stir more than just the Raven's imagination.

"It's probable that she's as homely as a sea slug," he said to himself, "but on the other hand, she may be as beautiful as the fronds of the hemlock would be against a bright spring sunrise, if only there were light enough to make one." And in that idle speculation, he found the solution to his problem.

He waited until the young woman, whose footsteps he could distinguish by now from those of her father, came to the river to gather water. Then he changed himself into a single hemlock needle, dropped himself into the river and floated down just in time to be caught in the basket which the girl was dipping in the river.

Even in his much diminished form, the Raven was able to make at least a very small magic—enough to make the girl so thirsty she took a deep drink from the basket, and in doing so, swallowed the needle.

The Raven slithered down deep into her insides and found a soft, comfortable spot, where he transformed himself once more, this time into a very small human being, and went to sleep for a long while. And as he slept he grew.

The young girl didn't have any idea what was happening to her, and of course she didn't tell her father, who noticed nothing unusual because it was so dark—until suddenly he became very aware indeed of a new presence in the house, as the Raven at last emerged triumphantly in the shape of a human boychild.

He was—or would have been, if anyone could have seen him—a strange-looking boy, with a long, beaklike nose and a few feathers here and there. In addition, he had the shining eyes of the Raven, which would have given his face a bright, inquisitive appearance—if anyone could have seen these features then.

And he was noisy. He had a cry that contained all the noises of a spoiled child and an angry raven—yet he could sometimes speak as softly as the wind in the hemlock boughs, with an echo of that beautiful other sound, like an organic bell, which is also part of every raven's speech.

At times like that his grandfather grew to love this strange new member of his household and spent many hours playing with him, making him toys and inventing games for him.

As he gained more and more of the affection and confidence of the old man, the Raven felt more intently around the house, trying to find where the light was hidden. After much exploration, he was convinced it was kept in the big box which stood in the corner of the house. One day he cautiously lifted the lid, but of course could see nothing, and all he could feel was another box. His grandfather, however, heard his precious treasure chest being disturbed, and he dealt very harshly with the would-be thief, threatening dire punishment if the Ravenchild ever touched the box again.

This triggered a tidal wave of noisy protests, followed by tender importuning, in which the Raven never mentioned the light, but only pleaded for the largest box. That box, said the Ravenchild, was the one thing he needed to make him completely happy.

As most if not all grandfathers have done since the beginning, the old man finally yielded and gave his grandchild the outermost box. This contented the boy for a short time—but as most if not all grandchildren have done since the beginning, the Raven soon demanded the next box.

It took many days and much cajoling, carefully balanced with well-planned tantrums, but one by one the boxes were removed. When only a few were left, a strange radiance, never before seen, began to infuse the darkness of the house, disclosing vague shapes and their shadows, still too dim to have definite form. The Ravenchild then begged in his most pitiful voice to be allowed to hold the light for just a moment.

His request was instantly refused, but of course in time his grandfather yielded. The old man lifted the light, in the form of a beautiful, incandescent ball, from the final box and tossed it to his grandson.

He had only a glimpse of the child on whom he had lavished such love and affection, for even as the light was travelling toward him, the child changed from his human form to a huge, shining black shadow, wings spread and beak open, waiting. The Raven snapped up the light in his jaws, thrust his great wings downward and shot through the smokehole of the house into the huge darkness of the world.

That world was at once transformed. Mountains and valleys were starkly silhouetted, the river sparkled with broken reflections, and everywhere life began to stir. And from far away, another great winged shape launched itself into the air, as light struck the eyes of the Eagle for the first time and showed him his target.

The Raven flew on, rejoicing in his wonderful new possession, admiring the effect it had on the world below, revelling in the experience of being able to see where he was going, instead of flying blind and hoping for the best. He was having such a good time that he never saw the Eagle until the Eagle was almost upon him. In a panic he swerved to escape the savage outstretched claws, and in doing so he dropped a good half of the light he was carrying. It fell to the rocky ground below and there broke into pieces—one large piece and too many small ones to count. They bounced back into the sky and remain there even today as the moon and the stars that glorify the night.

The Eagle pursued the Raven beyond the rim of the world, and there, exhausted by the long chase, the Raven finally let go of his last piece of light. Out beyond the rim of the world, it floated gently on the clouds and started up over the mountains lying to the east.

Its first rays caught the smokehole of the house by the river, where the old man sat weeping bitterly over the loss of his precious light and the treachery of his grandchild. But as the light reached in, he looked up and for the first time saw his daughter, who had been quietly sitting during all this time, completely bewildered by the rush of events.

The old man saw that she was as beautiful as the fronds of a hemlock against a spring sky at sunrise, and he began to feel a little better.

FIRST NIGHT

CHRISTOPHER DEWDNEY

Christopher Dewdney (1951–) is the son of artist and author Selwyn Dewdney, famous for documenting the native rock paintings of northern Ontario. The mix of art and science that marked Christopher's childhood nurtured an extraordinary body of poems, which led to his inclusion, together with William Burroughs, Allen Ginsberg, Michael Ondaatje, and Tom Waits, in the internationally acclaimed film *Poetry in Motion* (1984). A Renaissance man adept in many scientific and literary disciplines, Dewdney is also the author of *Acquainted with the Night: Excursions Through the World After Dark* (2004), a remarkable journey through the history and lore, philosophy and physics, sociology and culture of the night. In this excerpt, he debunks the myths of dark origins, revealing that our universe, in fact, began in light.

. . .

FOR THE FIRST few hundred thousand years of its existence, our universe consisted of glowing plasma—there was no darkness, only light. Then, as matter began forming out of

22

the plasma, gravity appeared, and soon dark, unlit patches of space began to proliferate within the cooling plasma. After that, the light in the universe went out completely and the universe entered a period of absolute darkness. This first (but not last) cosmic night lasted five hundred million years.

But within the darkness the universe was evolving, gravity began exerting its force, and the once-glowing plasma was slowly transforming into clouds of gas. Inside this utter blackness the embryos of stars and galaxies began to form. Eventually, at some point about fourteen billion years ago, the nuclear fires of an original star ignited and the first starlight shone in the darkness. More and more stars began to catch fire and eventually they formed the first galaxies. Gradually the dark space between these stars and galaxies became the largest part of the continuously expanding universe and provided the darkness necessary for a night sky. So the very first night in the universe occurred then, a little less than fourteen billion years ago, on a barren planet or asteroid orbiting the youngest star there ever was.

But what about the first night on earth? When did that occur? According to the scientific genesis, our own solar system was born approximately 4.6 billion years ago in a vast nebula of dust and gas afloat in the interstellar void. Perhaps initiated by the shock wave of a nearby exploding star, a section of the nebula began to collapse on itself in a runaway gravitational attraction. This nebula was incredibly massive, and as billions of tons of matter were condensed at its core, it began to spin from centrifugal force. Then, as had happened billions of times already in the past ten billion years, at the densest center of the cloud of dust and gas a red glow appeared, the beginning of a new star, our sun. Out of darkness, out of compressed interstellar dust, came light, and out of the disc of dust and gases spinning around the new sun came the planets.

So when was the first night on earth? Was the establishment of night and day a gradual process or an abrupt one? We can answer the first question roughly by looking at the history of our planet. The earth coalesced into its current shape, a slightly oblate spheroid, about 4.5 billion years ago, so the primary night had to have occurred sometime close to that, within, say, a few million years. Because night needs daylight to define it, night could only have started when sunlight reached the surface of our planet, after the dust of creation had been scrubbed from earth's sky. This was probably a gradual process and possibly so incremental that it would be hard to pinpoint the first night exactly. (Perhaps, though, it might have been a faster-paced event. A recent lunar theory proposed by Japanese astrophysicist Eiichiro Kokubo suggests that the moon's original dust cloud was cleared away within a month of the moon's formation. It's possible the same thing happened on earth, and perhaps there really was an initial sunset after which the stars shone in a clear night sky for the first time.)

What we do know is that the first night wasn't very long. The earth was spinning much faster then, before the moon put the brakes on. The gravitational interaction of the earth and the moon slows the earth's rotation by about two milliseconds each century, twenty seconds per million years, and two hours every three hundred and eighty million years. About nine hundred million years ago, for example, there were four hundred and eighty-one eighteen-hour days in a year, and the average night was only nine hours long. (Interestingly enough, these estimates have been verified by paleontology. Three-hundred-and-seventy-million-year-old fossil corals have four hundred daily growth rings in one yearly cycle, exactly the number of days predicted by the formula!)

If you could travel back in time a billion years, the earth would appear very different. There would be rivers and mountains and deserts, but no land plants. Aquatic life was well established by then, though the creatures that were large enough to be seen would look so strange that you'd think you were on an alien planet. At night, looking up at the stars, you'd see none of today's constellations. That might be somewhat disconcerting, but even more disconcerting would be the speed of the moonrise. A visibly larger moon (it was once much closer to the earth) would seem to leap up from the horizon, and as it crossed the night sky, its pace would be noticeably faster; in fact, it would appear to literally sail through the stars. But to experience the first night on our planet, we'd have to travel even farther back in time, much farther, billions of years before the beginning of life.

If we extend the same formula for calculating the length of the day back to the very beginning of the earth, 4.5 billion years ago, it shows the first night (after the dust had been cleared from the earth's sky) would have lasted only minutes! The stars would appear to wheel dizzily through the heavens and the moon, if there were one (according to a recent theory the moon was created by a large asteroid impact a few million years after the formation of the earth), would careen through the stars like a cannonball. The centrifugal force of such a rapidly spinning earth would be enough to make you lightfooted, but you probably wouldn't notice it, because the red-hot, molten surface and toxic atmosphere would require asbestos snowshoes and a flame-retardant spacesuit.

Nights are thankfully much more serene now, and the pace of the twelve-hour night described in this book seems languorous in comparison with those first frenetic evenings. Looking billions of years into the future of our solar system, physicists predict that the pace of the earth's spin will eventually slow until it stops, and night will be frozen on one side of the planet. It will be a very cold night on a very inhospitable earth. But it is unlikely humans will be around, at least in their present form, to take in the spectacle. For interstellar night beckons us, and we have already flown through the deep night of space to the moon.

SHADOW WORLD

DIANE ACKERMAN

Diane Ackerman (1948–) did her PhD in English at Cornell University under Carl Sagan. Since then, a combination of science and literature has infused her writing. She has published eight poetry collections, two children's books, and eleven works of nonfiction, including *The Zookeeper's Wife* (2007), which won the Orion Book Award, conferred annually to a work that deepens the human connection with nature. *A Natural History of the Senses* (1990), excerpted here, brought Ackerman to public prominence. Later made into a PBS series, it exemplifies her quirky, poetic take on the natural world. "Look at your feet," she writes. "You are standing in the sky. When we think of the sky, we tend to look up, but the sky actually begins at the earth."

. . .

IT IS NIGHTTIME on the planet Earth. But that is only a whim of nature, a result of our planet rolling in space at 1,000 miles per minute. What we call "night" is the time we spend facing the secret reaches of space, where other solar systems and, perhaps, other planetarians dwell. Don't think of night as the absence of day; think of it as a kind of freedom. Turned away from our sun, we see the dawning of far-flung galaxies. We are no longer sun-blind to the star-coated universe we inhabit. The endless black, which seems to stretch forever between the stars and even backwards in time to the Big Bang, we call "infinity," from the French *in-fini*, meaning unfinished or incomplete. Night is a shadow world. The only shadows we see at night are cast by the moonlight, or by artificial light, but night itself is a shadow.

In the country, you can see more stars, and the night looks like an upside-down well that deepens forever. If you're patient and wait until your eyes adjust to the darkness, you can see the Milky Way as a creamy smudge across the sky. Just as different cultures have connected the stars into different constellations, they've seen their own private dramas in the Milky Way. The "backbone of night" the Bushmen of the Kalahari call it. To the Swedes, it is the "winter street" leading to heaven. To the Hebridean islanders, the "pathway of the secret people." To the Norse, the "path of ghosts." To the Patagonians, obsessed with their flightless birds, "the White Pampas where ghosts hunt rheas." But in the city you can see the major constellations more easily because there are fewer stars visible to distract you.

Wherever you are, the best way to watch stars is lying on your back. Tonight the half-moon has a Mayan profile. It looks luminous and shimmery, a true beacon in the night, and yet I know its brilliance is all borrowed light. By day, if I held a mirror and bounced a spot of sunlight around the trees, I would be mimicking how the moon reflects light, having none of its own to give. Above me, between Sagittarius and Aquarius, the constellation Capricorn ambles across the sky. The Aztecs pictured it as a whale *(cipactli)*, the East Indians saw an antelope *(makaram)*, the Greeks labeled it "the gate of the gods," and to the Assyrians it was a goat-fish *(munaxa)*. Perhaps the best-known star in the world is the North Star, or Polaris, though of course it has many other names; to the Navaho, it is "The Star That Does Not Move," to the Chinese, the "Great Imperial Ruler of Heaven."

Throughout time, people have looked up at the sky to figure out where they were. When I was a girl, I used to take an empty can, stretch a piece of tinfoil over one end and pierce pinholes in it in the outline of a constellation; then I'd shine a flashlight in the other end, and have my own private planetarium. How many wanderers, lost on land or sea, have waited till night to try and chart their way home with help from the North Star. Locating it as they did connects us across time to those early nomads. First you find the Big Dipper and extend a line through the outer two stars of its ladle. Then you'll see that the North Star looks like a dollop of cream fallen from the upside-down Dipper. If the Big Dipper isn't visible, you can find the North Star by looking for Cassiopeia, a constellation just below Polaris that's shaped like a W or an M, depending on the time you see it. To me, it usually looks like a butterfly. Because the Earth revolves, the stars seem to drift from east to west across the sky, so another way to tell direction is to keep your eye on one bright star in particular; if it appears to rise, then you're facing east. If it seems to be falling, you're facing west. When I was a Girl Scout, we found our direction during the day by putting a straight stick in the ground. Then we'd go about our business for a few hours and return when the stick cast a shadow about six inches long. The sun would have moved west, and the shadow would be pointing east. Sometimes we used a wristwatch as a compass: Place the watch face up, with the hour hand pointing toward the sun. Pick up a pine needle or twig and hold it upright at the edge of the dial so that it casts a shadow along the hour hand. South will be halfway between the hour hand and twelve o'clock. There are many other ways to tell direction, of course, since roaming is one of the things human beings love to do best—but only if they can count on getting home safely. If you see a tree standing out in the open, with heavy moss on one side, that side is probably north, since moss grows heaviest on the shadiest side of a tree. If you see a tree stump, its rings will probably be thicker on the sunny side, or south. You can also look up at the tops of pine trees, which mainly point east. Or, if you happen to know where the prevailing wind is coming from, you can read direction from the wind-bent grasses.

It's November. The Leonids are due in Leo. Pieces of comet that fall mainly after sunset or before sunrise, they appear in the same constellations each year at the same time. In Antarctica, I had hoped to see auroras, veils of light caused by the solar wind bumping into the earth's magnetic field and leaving a gorgeous shimmer behind. But our days were mainly sun-perfect, and our nights a grisly gray twilight. In the evening, the sea looked like pounded gunmetal, but there were no auroras to make glitter paths overhead. Here is how Captain Robert Scott described one display in June 1911:

> The eastern sky was massed with swaying auroral light . . . fold on fold the arches and curtains of vibrating luminosity rose and spread across the sky, to slowly face and yet again spring to glowing life.
>
> The brighter light seemed to flow, now to mass itself in wreathing folds in one quarter, from which lustrous streamers shot upward, and anon to run in waves through the system of some dimmer figure.
>
> It is impossible to witness such a beautiful phenomenon without a sense of awe, and yet this sentiment is not inspired by its brilliancy but rather by its delicacy in light and colour, its transparency, and above all by its tremulous evanescence of form.

Tonight Mars glows like a steady red ember. Though only a dot of light in the sky, it is in my mind a place of blustery plains, volcanoes, rift valleys, sand dunes, wind-carved arches, dry river beds, and brilliant white polar caps that wax and wane with the seasons. There may even have been a climate there once, and running water. Soon Venus will appear as a bright silvery light, as it usually does about three hours after sunset or before sunrise. With its gauzy white face, it looks mummified in photos, but I know that impression is given by cloud banks full of acids floating above a surface where tricks of light abound and the temperatures are hot enough to melt lead. There are many kinds of vision—literal, imaginative, hallucinatory; visions of greatness or of great possibilities. Although I can't see the steady light of other planets just yet, I know they are there all the same, along with the asteroids, comets, distant galaxies, neutron stars, black holes, and other phantoms of deep space. And I picture them with a surety Walt Whitman understood when he proclaimed: "The bright suns I see and the dark suns I cannot see are in their place."

NAVIGATING THE
NIGHTSCAPE

A. ROGER EKIRCH

A Roger Ekirch (1950–) is a professor of history at Virginia Polytech-nic Institute, where he has written on subjects ranging from North Carolina society to the British transportation of convicts to the colonies. *At Day's Close: Night in Times Past* (2005), the source of this passage, brought Ekirch international recognition. Named a best book of the year by the *Observer, Discover* magazine, and Amazon.com, *At Day's Close* explores the history of nighttime in Western society prior to the Industrial Revolution. The night, long ignored by historians and anthropologists alike, is, Ekirch argues, more than the forgotten half of human existence; it embodies its own distinct culture. The book opens with a telling epigraph from Thomas Tryon: "Let the night teach us what we are, and the day what we should be."

· · ·

OBSERVERS AS EARLY as Aristotle and Lucretius have com-mented upon the timidity of young children at night. According to psychologists, around two years of age the young first exhibit an instinctive fear of the dark. Anxieties, dormant since birth, are awakened by a rising awareness of the outside world. There is no reason to think that this standard pattern of childhood development was any different in premodern communities. The ancient Spartans reputedly made their sons spend entire evenings among the tombs to conquer their fears. "Men feare death as children feare to goe in the dark," observed Francis Bacon.

In early modern times, youthful fears, in parents' eyes, often served a salutary purpose. Rather than soothe children's anxieties, adults routinely reinforced them through tales of the supernatural, in part bearing testimony to their own apprehensions. "That natural fear in children is increased with tales," Bacon noted. Of "our mothers maids," the Elizabethan author Reginald Scot described, "they have so fraied us with bull beggars, spirits, witches, urchens, elves, hags, fairies . . . that we are afraid of our owne shadowes." There were also narratives involving kidnappers, murderers, and thieves. As a girl in seventeenth-century Ghent, Isabella de Moerloose was frightened by the story of "the man with the long coat, of whom it was said that he looked for firstborn children" to kill. The specter of a one-eyed soldier in the royal guard was used to discipline Louis XIII of France (1601–1643) as a child. By warning of bogeymen that preyed on naughty youngsters, parents and servants, critics alleged, played upon children's worst fears to compel obedience. "As soon as one tries to still a child," complained the Dutch author Jacob Cats, "one introduces a variety of bizarre features: a ghost, a bogeyman, a lifeless spirit."

Some parents, as punishment, confined children to dark closets or impersonated evil sprits. A Dutch father, Constantijn Huygens, used a doll dressed in black to threaten his infant daughter. The father of Philippe de Strozzi in sixteenth-century France knocked on his chamber door one night. "Disguising his voice in a horrible manner," the father hoped to test his son's courage. Philippe passed the test. Struck on the forehead, his father was forced to retreat, "swearing to never again frighten him in this way at night."

Examples like these offer ample fodder for those historians who have depicted the early modern family in a harsh light, as a repressive institution devoid of human affection. To draw that connection here, however, would be to miss a larger point. Although used as an occasional tool of discipline, storytelling and bogeymen served an important educational function. At night, most of all, young children needed to be put on guard. Tales, along with ballads and proverbs, afforded a customary means in this largely illiterate age of imparting cautionary advice. Thus in *Traité de l'Education des Filles* (1687), the French churchman Fénelon described nurses who gave "children stupid fears of ghosts and spirits," thereby exercising their own judgment "as to the things" infants "should seek after or avoid." Similarly, a visitor to Sicily wrote of "superstitious parents, nurses, and others such like teachers" who spread tales of witchcraft. There was nothing impersonal or abstract about most stories. Many recounted the terrible deeds of neighborhood ghosts and witches, taking care to identify spots that children at night should avoid. According to Jean Paul, his father, a schoolmaster, "did not spare us a single apparition or foolery, which he had ever heard of or believed to have met with, himself." In contrast to most adults, however, his father "combined with a firm belief in them the equally firm courage to face them."

Central, also, to children's education was their progressive exposure to darkness. Collecting firewood, gathering berries, and tending livestock all took youths outdoors in the evening. The engraver Thomas Bewick, growing up in Northumberland, was sent by his father on "any errand in the night." "Perhaps," he reflected as an adult, "my being frequently exposed to being alone in the dark" helped to lessen the terror. Some tasks were contrived. In 1748, the author of *Dialogues on the Passions, Habits, and Affections Peculiar to Children* advised parents: "You must create little errands, as if by accident, to send him in the dark, but such as can take up but little time; and encrease the length of time by degrees, as you find his courage encrease." The son of a shoemaker, young Thomas Holcroft was sent one night to a distant farm. "Now and then making a false step," he remembered later of the route. With his father and a companion secretly following at a distance, the lad completed his journey unscathed. "At last I got safely home, glad to be rid of my fears, and inwardly not a little elated with my success."

Games served the same purpose. Rousseau urged reliance on "night games" for children, including a complex labyrinth formed by tables and chairs. "Accustomed to having a good footing in darkness, practiced at handling with ease all surrounding bodies," he observed, "his feet and hands will lead him without difficulty in the deepest darkness." Outdoor contests, such as "Fox and Hounds," were designed for the obscurity of night. Restif de la Bretonne, as a boy, enjoyed the contest of "Wolf," which in his French village "was always played in the dark," as in parts of Britain was "Bogle about the Stacks," a game that allowed children to act out their fears of ghosts. A favorite throughout the British Isles was "Can I Get There by Candle Light?" Dating to the sixteenth century, if not earlier, one version of the game pitted a coven of "witches" against a larger band of "travelers." Although not intended for the dark, the game conveyed two practical lessons: the importance of returning home, when possible, before "candle-lighting"; and the need to beware of sinister forces once night fell. "Watch out!" chanted the players, "mighty bad witches on the road tonight."

Some youngsters, like Jonathan Martin, were impatient learners. The son of a Northumberland forester, he routinely absconded from bed on summer nights to ramble alone in the woods. One morning, finally, he was returned home by men who had first taken the six-year-old for a ghost. His father, alert to the dangers of such rash behavior, immediately forbade Jonathan's solitary excursions. Both at home and abroad, prudence after nightfall was essential. It was one thing to invade night's dominion; it was quite another to flout its laws.

BEGINNINGS

TIMOTHY FERRIS

Timothy Ferris (1944–) has been gazing at the night sky for fifty years. A former newspaper reporter, he has turned his passion for the stars into twelve books, including *Coming of Age in the Milky Way* (1988) and *The Whole Shebang* (1997). *Seeing in the Dark: How Backyard Stargazers Are Probing Deep Space and Guarding Earth from Interplanetary Peril* (2002), from which this selection is taken, is part memoir, part reportage. In it, Ferris reveals the genesis of his obsession and ponders a science in which amateurs still make significant contributions. In the PBS documentary of the same name, Ferris bemoans the brightening of the urban night, lauding communities that are turning off their lights. "There is hope that we can make the starry sky once again a legacy to our children."

. . .

AT DAWN ON a deserted Florida beach in 1954, the first rays of the Sun sent my father's long shadow and my shorter one rippling like kite tails across the rumpled sands. We were out early to see what had washed up during the night. In the past we'd found a gleaming conch shell that whispered surf sounds like betrayed secrets; a dark, ancient wine bottle, stout and heavy as a stonecutter's mallet; and a bottle with a note in it from an English schoolgirl who tossed it from the taffrail of a cruise ship in the Bahamas, a hundred miles away. The previous winter a freighter burned and sank in the Gulf Stream, and for weeks afterward cases of its cargo washed up, providing us with a set of new wooden lawn furniture.

The rising Sun painted the seashore gold, lighting up the pear-amber flotation balls clustered in tangles of seaweed, the indigo sails of beached Portuguese men-of-war, and the miles of unbroken Australian pines that stretched south along the beach. My father in his faded swim trunks was golden, too. He'd been a boxer and a tennis pro, had grown fat and famous in the café society of prewar San Juan and Miami Beach, then gone broke and gone to work driving a truck. Now he looked like an athlete again, tanned and muscled, given to drawing lines on the beach so we could practice the standing broad jump and the hundred-yard dash. Weekdays he loaded forty-pound cement bags onto a flatbed truck and drove them to construction sites. On weekends he delivered wooden cases of soft drinks to gas stations and bait shops in the Everglades. Nights and early mornings, he sat at a typewriter propped on the rattan table in our tiny living room, writing short stories that he sold to magazines for "extra" money. He'd stopped drinking when we fled the city, had escaped the boredom that stalked him when his name was in the gossip columns, and was full of wit and wonder.

"Look," he said, touching my left arm lightly to bring me to a halt as we stepped gingerly around a delta fan of violet men-of-war tentacles. Up ahead, high on the beach, something strange was happening—a slow flurry in the sand, rhythmic and methodical. We advanced slowly, peering intently, trying to make sense of it. Scoops of sand flopped up and over, casting long shadows.

"It's a sea turtle," he whispered. "A loggerhead, I think. She's been laying her eggs."

Now I saw her—the enormous shell, so dusted with sand that it had been nearly invisible, and the big, powerful flippers, throwing sand into the hole beneath. My father explained that she had dug the hole five or six feet deep, laid something like a hundred eggs in it, and now was covering it up to keep them safe from predators. We backed away and watched as the turtle finished her labors. Then she heaved her gigantic form down to the shoreline and sank beneath the waves, her fins leaving strange, deep tracks on the beach.

My father found two fallen palm branches, handed one to me, and we swept the sand to erase the tracks, taking care not to step on the nest and pack it down, as this might hinder the little turtles when they hatched and clawed their way to the top. "It's against the law to dig up turtle eggs, but people do it anyway," he said, as we brushed. "If the nest is left alone, the baby turtles will dig their way out in a month or two and head straight back to sea. I don't know how they find the water, or get along on their own out there, but at least some of them must manage it or there wouldn't be any more sea turtles. Was it a full Moon last night?"

"I'm not sure."

"May have been. It's June, and they say loggerheads like to lay their eggs at the first full Moon in June. The tides are higher then, so the sea covers up more of the mother's tracks. But you'd think she'd prefer the dark of the Moon. They're usually done laying by dawn. This one was a bit late."

"How do they know when it's a full Moon—and the right full Moon?"

"I don't know. A female loggerhead can wander from here to the Azores and find her way back to the same beach where she was hatched when it's time to lay her eggs. Possibly they navigate by sensing the Earth's magnetic field lines."

OUR LIFE on this all-but-deserted coast was a species of economic exile, punctuated by the petty embarrassments that afflict the poor. Each morning I siphoned gasoline from the gas tank of our used car to prime the carburetor so it would start, then with the taste of petrol in my mouth took a small yellow bus to an abject school where I was regarded as well off because I wore shoes and a shirt. (To this day I burn with humiliation at the memory of having been thoughtless enough to ask a classmate, "Gabe, how come you don't wear shoes to school?" to which he replied in a wire-taut Appalachian drawl, "May-be if ah *hay-ed* some shoes, ah would *way-aire the*-em.") At the market my mother took groceries back from the checkout counter when we hadn't the money to pay for them all, and through my flimsy bedroom door I could hear the strain in her voice as she contended with the landlord about when we would pay the rent.

But we lived in a beautiful part of this world. Our little house looked out across a windswept field of sea grape to the blue-green sea. At night the stars stood out so vividly that they seemed to crackle, and we would watch, transfixed, as the Moon rose the color of a blood orange, then changed into costumes of ermine and silver. My brother, Bruce, and I fell asleep each night to the subdued hiss and thunder of the waves—all alike, yet no two identical—and awoke to the same ceaselessly inventive sounds each morning, and did not understand that we were poor, and imagined that we were blessed . . .

The night skies over Key Biscayne in those days were inky dark and rock steady. The stars seemed close at hand, like the spangles inside a princely Bedouin tent. I learned the constellations from a book called *The Stars: A New Way to See Them*, written by H.A. Rey, coauthor and illustrator of the "Curious George" books. I would take a dining-room chair out to the front lawn, illuminate Rey's books with a little flashlight whose lens I'd painted with my mother's red nail polish, and trace the outlines of mighty Orion, Cygnus the swan flying south in the Milky Way, and the almost frightening Scorpius, swollen to gigantic size in the briny air along the southern horizon, its starry stinger lurking above the palm fronds.

Mars loomed in the east like a garnet out of Araby, getting brighter every night. I'd read that it was approaching opposition, the point when Earth lay in a direct line from Mars to the Sun so that the planets were close together, and that the opposition this year, 1956, was to be an especially favorable one. Mars would draw within 36 million miles of Earth, affording exceptional views of its polar caps and continent-like markings and prompting fresh debate over the reality of the famous canals, which the astronomer Percival Lowell believed to have been built by an ancient and parched civilization to ferry water to their cities from the poles. But to see these wonders required a telescope. I found a suitably cheap one in a tiny advertisement in the back of *Popular Mechanics,* and my parents gave it to me as an early Christmas present that fall.

Stargazers, like musicians, typically learn on inferior instruments, and my first telescope was suitably wretched. It consisted of a skinny tube made of Bakelite—a brittle and literally tacky substance that, like yogurt, is easier to recognize than to describe—mounted irresolutely atop a spindly tripod fashioned from wood so green that its legs bowed inward under their own meager weight. Into one end of the tube was glued a war-surplus objective lens with a diameter of 1.6 inches, giving it less light-gathering power than an ordinary pair of reading glasses. The other end held a cardboard eyepiece; you changed the magnifying power by taking it apart and reassembling its yellowing lenses into various bewildering combinations.

Nobody else could see much of anything through this telescope, nor did I have a great deal of initial success, lacking experience as I did—and having been a bit unnerved when, on one of my first attempts to use the thing, I looked through its four-power finder scope and was confronted by the grotesquely magnified image of a flying cockroach who had just landed on the tube and was scurrying my way. But I could see Mars—its polar caps, at least, and a few of the most distinct surface markings, especially the dark dagger shape of the northern hemisphere feature Syrtis Major—and the effect was transforming. Mars was, after all, a world, and even more mysterious then than it is today. Staying up late on cold, clear nights, out in the front yard watching Mars, I began to learn how to observe a planet. I came to realize that the air is rather like the lens of the eye, a curved membrane thinnest at its center—the zenith—and thicker toward the sides. That's why the sky on a sunny day looks deep blue overhead and pallid near the horizon, and it means that planets are seen most clearly when highest in the sky. I learned that the highest powers of magnification do not necessarily produce the best results: Instead, for any given telescope, trained on a given object at a given time and place, there is an ideal power, a sweet spot. Once you've found it, the trick is to keep watching, waiting for moments when turbulence settles out of the air and the eye is treated to a gratifying and tantalizing instant of clarity—an instant as fleeting, yet as potentially significant, as the flash of insight that brings an original idea . . .

Some of my friends got telescopes for themselves. The ablest observer among them was Charles Ray Goodwin III, a boy of sufficient seriousness of mind that he was teaching himself Russian so that he could read Solzhenitsyn in the original. Chuck and I learned from books how to make drawings of the Moon and the planets with charcoal and colored pencils. Later we got hold of a couple of old cameras and took time-exposure photographs that recorded the lurid orange hue of the eclipsed Moon and the tangle of gas clouds that engulf the constellation Orion. A few of us formed a club—the Key Biscayne Astronomical Association, or KBAA—with Chuck as president, and started keeping observing logs, portentously filling them with sketches and data like those we'd seen in the books of the august, full-grown members of the British Astronomical Association . . .

As happens if you spend a lot of time outdoors at night, we encountered some unexpected spectacles. One night we saw a mighty fireball—a meteor, a chunk of rock probably no bigger than a golf ball but spectacular when seen hurtling into Earth's atmosphere and burning up from friction with the air. I was bending to fetch a star chart from the lawn when suddenly the colors of the chart leaped into view—the blue of the Milky Way and the red oval galaxies on the white page, laid against an abruptly vivid carpet of bright green grass. I looked up and saw the whole neighborhood bathed in something approaching sunlight, with green coconut palms waving against a blue sky. Everything cast two shadows, one black and one red, and the shadows were shifting, clocking rapidly from north to south. In the sky I saw the fireball itself, silver and yellow with a red halo and brighter than the Moon, racing northwest and leaving behind a fading white trail flecked with gold.

Watching it fade I recalled a day, years earlier, when my mother had gone into a little rural grocery and I'd wandered over to the railroad crossing. All was quiet. The twilight sky was lavender and dark enough that Venus was out, hung above a freshly minted sickle Moon. Then the crossing-gate alarm gong started ringing, the big red lamps flashed, and the black-and-white-striped gates went down, blocking the dirt road. There was no train in sight, but the rails began to hum. I fished a penny from my pocket, laid it on the track, and dashed back a safe distance, having been warned that if you stood too close to a speeding train it could suck you in under the wheels. A yellow headlamp appeared in the distance and closed with incredible speed. The train flashed past—an express!—and shot through in a blast of noise, going so fast that my eye could capture only a few snapshots in the blur. There were tan cars with a blood-red stripe that rose from the diesel engine's bullet snout and extended down the cars under their windows, in the warm yellow light of which I thought I caught a glimpse of dining tables covered in white linen. Then the train was gone, in a waft of vacuum that sent sheets of newsprint spiraling in the warm, moist air.

I stood there frozen, my jaw agape, staring after it. I'd been wearing a black cardboard cowboy hat and found that I'd taken it off and was holding it over my heart. Years later I heard an old recording by the Mississippi blues singer Bukka White that captured the sensation:

> Got that fast special streamline,
> Leaving out of Memphis, Tennessee,
> Going into New Orleans.

Be runnin' so fast the hoboes don't fool with that train,
They just stand by the track
With their hats in their hands . . .
Play it lonesome, now, 'cause I'm a hobo myself sometimes.

Visions like this one produced a sensation that I did not know how to express until, years later, I read what Einstein had to say about the lesson he'd learned from his first encounter with geometry, which, he recalled, provided a way "to free myself from the chains of the 'merely-personal,' from an existence which is dominated by wishes, hopes, and primitive feelings. Out yonder there was this huge world, which exists independently of us human beings and which stands before us like a great, eternal riddle, at least partially accessible to our inspection and thinking. The contemplation of this world beckoned like a liberation."

Decades later, back in Key Biscayne to give a talk, I found that its once-dark skies had been turned to fish-gray by urban lights. Efforts were under way to reduce the light pollution, by limiting the size of advertising signs and encouraging the use of hooded lamps that illuminate the ground without wasting energy on the sky. The stargazers working on the light-pollution issue had found allies among marine biologists concerned with nesting sea turtles. The turtles, it seems, prefer their beaches dark at night.

TOTAL ECLIPSE

ANNIE DILLARD

Annie Dillard (1945–) is one of America's most original and incisive writers of narrative nonfiction. She came to international attention when
her second book, *Pilgrim at Tinker Creek* (1974), won the Pulitzer Prize.
She has written six other books of nonfiction as well as two collections of
poetry, two novels, and a memoir, *An American Childhood* (1987), about
growing up in Pittsburgh. Obsessed by the minutiae of nature and the
grand metaphysical questions it provokes, Dillard says of herself, "I am no
scientist. I am a wanderer with a background in theology and a penchant
for quirky facts." In this piece from her 1982 collection of essays, *Teaching
a Stone to Talk*, Dillard explores the absence of light that is a total eclipse—
a night that falls suddenly at midday.

. . .

IT WAS BEFORE dawn when we found a highway out of town
and drove into the unfamiliar countryside. By the growing
light we could see a band of cirrostratus clouds in the sky. Later

the rising sun would clear these clouds before the eclipse began. We drove at random until we came to a range of unfenced hills. We pulled off the highway, bundled up, and climbed one of these hills.

The hill was five hundred feet high. Long winter-killed grass covered it, as high as our knees. We climbed and rested, sweating in the cold; we passed clumps of bundled people on the hillside who were setting up telescopes and fiddling with cameras. The top of the hill stuck up in the middle of the sky. We tightened our scarves and looked around.

East of us rose another hill like ours. Between the hills, far below, was the highway which threaded south into the valley. This was the Yakima valley; I had never seen it before. It is justly famous for its beauty, like every planted valley. It extended south into the horizon, a distant dream of a valley, a Shangri-la. All its hundreds of low, golden slopes bore orchards. Among the orchards were towns, and roads, and plowed and fallow fields. Through the valley wandered a thin, shining river; from the river extended fine, frozen irrigation ditches. Distance blurred and blued the sight, so that the whole valley looked like a thickness or sediment at the bottom of the sky. Directly behind us was more sky, and empty lowlands blued by distance, and Mount Adams. Mount Adams was an enormous, snow-covered volcanic cone rising flat, like so much scenery.

Now the sun was up. We could not see it; but the sky behind the band of clouds was yellow, and, far down the valley, some hillside orchards had lighted up. More people were parking near the highway and climbing the hills. It was the West. All of us rugged individualists were wearing knit caps and blue nylon parkas. People were climbing the nearby hills and setting up ·shop in clumps among the dead grasses. It looked as though we had all gathered on hilltops to pray for the world on its last day. It looked as though we had all crawled out of spaceships and were preparing to assault the valley below. It looked as though we were scattered on hilltops at dawn to sacrifice virgins, make rain, set stone stelae in a ring. There was no place out of the wind. The straw grasses banged our legs.

Up in the sky where we stood the air was lusterless yellow. To the west the sky was blue. Now the sun cleared the clouds. We cast rough shadows on the blowing grass; freezing, we waved our arms. Near the sun the sky was bright and colorless. There was nothing to see.

IT BEGAN with no ado. It was odd that such a well-advertised public event should have no starting gun, no overture, no introductory speaker. I should have known right then that I was out of my depth. Without pause or preamble, silent as orbits, a piece of the sun went away. We looked at it through welders' goggles. A piece of the sun was missing; in its place we saw empty sky.

I had seen a partial eclipse in 1970. A partial eclipse is very interesting. It bears almost no relation to a total eclipse. Seeing a partial eclipse bears the same relation to seeing a total eclipse as kissing a man does to marrying him, or as flying in an airplane does to falling out of an airplane. Although the one experience precedes the other, it in no way prepares you for it. During a partial eclipse the sky does not darken—not even when 94 percent of the sun is hidden. Nor does the sun, seen color-less through protective devices, seem terribly strange. We have all seen a sliver of light in the sky; we have all seen the cres-cent moon by day. However, during a partial eclipse the air does indeed get cold, precisely as if someone were standing between you and the fire. And blackbirds do fly back to their roosts. I had seen a partial eclipse before, and here was another.

What you see in an eclipse is entirely different from what you know. It is especially different for those of us whose grasp of astronomy is so frail that, given a flashlight, a grapefruit, two oranges, and fifteen years, we still could not figure out which way to set the clocks for Daylight Saving Time. Usually it is a bit of a trick to keep your knowledge from blinding you. But during an eclipse it is easy. What you see is much more convinc-ing than any wild-eyed theory you may know.

You may read that the moon has something to do with eclipses. I have never seen the moon yet. You do not see the moon. So near the sun, it is as completely invisible as the stars are by day. What you see before your eyes is the sun going through phases. It gets narrower and narrower, as the waning moon does, and, like the ordinary moon, it travels alone in the simple sky. The sky is of course background. It does not appear to eat the sun; it is far behind the sun. The sun simply shaves away; gradually, you see less sun and more sky.

THE SKY'S blue was deepening, but there was no darkness. The sun was a wide crescent, like a segment of tangerine. The wind freshened and blew steadily over the hill. The eastern hill across the highway grew dusky and sharp. The towns and orchards in the valley to the south were dissolving into the blue light. Only the thin river held a trickle of sun.

Now the sky to the west deepened to indigo, a color never seen. A dark sky usually loses color. This was a saturated, deep indigo, up in the air. Stuck up into that unworldly sky was the cone of Mount Adams, and the alpenglow was upon it. The alpenglow is that red light of sunset which holds out on snowy mountaintops long after the valleys and tablelands are dimmed. "Look at Mount Adams," I said, and that was the last sane moment I remember.

I TURNED back to the sun. It was going. The sun was going, and the world was wrong. The grasses were wrong; they were platinum. Their every detail of stem, head, and blade shone lightless and artificially distinct as an art photographer's platinum print. This color has never been seen on earth. The hues were metallic; their finish was matte. The hillside was a nineteenth-century tinted photograph from which the tints had faded. All the people you see in the photograph, distinct and detailed as their faces look, are now dead. The sky was navy blue. My hands were silver. All the distant hills' grasses were finespun metal which the wind laid down. I was watching a faded color print of a movie filmed in the Middle Ages; I was standing in it, by some mistake. I was standing in a movie of hillside grassed filmed in the

Middle Ages. I missed my own century, the people I knew, and the real light of day.

I looked at Gary. He was in the film. Everything was lost. He was a platinum print, a dead artist's version of life. I saw on his skull the darkness of night mixed with the colors of May. My mind was going out; my eyes were receding the way galaxies recede to the rim of space. Gary was light-years away, gesturing inside a circle of darkness, down the wrong end of a telescope. He smiled as if he saw me; the stringy crinkles around his eyes moved. The sight of him, familiar and wrong, was something I was remembering from centuries hence, from the other side of death: yes, *that* is the way he used to look, when we were living. When it was our generation's turn to be alive. I could not hear him; the wind was too loud. Behind him the sun was going. We had all started down the chute of time. At first it was pleasant; now there was no stopping it. Gary was chuting away across space, moving and talking and catching my eye, chuting down the long corridor of separation. The skin on his face moved like thin bronze plating that would peel.

The grass at our feet was wild barley. It was the wild einkorn wheat which grew on the hilly flanks of the Zagros Mountains, above the Euphrates valley, above the valley of the river we called *River*. We harvested the grass with stone sickles, I remember. We found the grasses on the hillsides; we built our shelter beside them and cut them down. That is how he used to look then, that one, moving and living and catching my eye, with the sky so dark behind him, and the wind blowing. God save our life.

FROM ALL the hills came screams. A piece of sky beside the crescent sun was detaching. It was a loosened circle of evening sky, suddenly lighted from the back. It was an abrupt black body out of nowhere; it was a flat disk; it was almost over the sun. That is when there were screams. At once this disk of sky slid over the sun like a lid. The sky snapped over the sun like a lens cover. The hatch in the brain slammed. Abruptly it was dark night, on the land and in the sky. In the night sky was a tiny ring of light. The hole where the sun belongs is very small. A thin ring of light marked its place. There was no sound. The eyes dried, the arteries drained, the lungs hushed. There was no world. We were the world's dead people rotating and orbiting around and around, embedded in the planet's crust, while the earth rolled down. Our minds were light-years distant, forgetful of almost everything. Only an extraordinary act of will could recall to us our former, living selves and our contexts in matter and time. We had, it seems, loved the planet and loved our lives, but could no longer remember the way of them. We got the light wrong. In the sky was something that should not be there. In the black sky was a ring of light. It was a thin ring, an old, thin silver wedding band, an old, worn ring. It was an old wedding band in the sky, or a morsel of bone. There were stars. It was all over.

DE STELLA NOVA

TYCHO BRAHE

Tycho Brahe (1546–1601) was the last major astronomer to observe the night sky without a telescope. Drawn early to stargazing, he wrote at seventeen, "I have studied all available charts of the planets and stars and none of them match the others. What's needed is a long-term project with the aim of mapping the heavens conducted from a single location." This he did, cataloging over a thousand stars, observations that Johannes Kepler used to construct his enduring laws of planetary movement. Significant among this Danish nobleman's sightings was a star that appeared unexpectedly in the constellation of Cassiopeia, thus refuting the Aristotelian worldview that the heavens beyond the moon's orbit were perfect and unchanging. Tycho's report, *De Stella Nova* (1573), excerpted here, coined the term "nova," meaning a new star.

. . .

Last year [1572], in the month of November, on the eleventh day of that month, in the evening, after sunset, when, according to my habit, I was contemplating the stars in a clear sky, I noticed that a new and unusual star, surpassing the other stars in brilliancy, was shining almost directly above my head; and since I had, almost from boyhood, known all the stars of the heavens perfectly (there is no great difficulty in attaining that knowledge), it was quite evident to me that there had never before been any star in that place in the sky, even the smallest, to say nothing of a star so conspicuously bright as this. I was so astonished at this sight that I was not ashamed to doubt the trustworthiness of my own eyes. But when I observed that others, too, on having the place pointed out to them, could see that there was really a star there, I had no further doubts.

A miracle indeed, either the greatest of all that have occurred in the whole range of nature since the beginning of the world, or one certainly that is to be classed with those attested by the Holy Oracles, the staying of the Sun in its course in answer to the prayers of Joshua, and the darkening of the Sun's face at the time of the Crucifixion. For all philosophers agree, and facts clearly prove it to be the case, that in the ethereal region of the celestial world no change, in the way either of generation or of corruption, takes place; but that the heavens and the celestial bodies in the heavens are without increase or diminution, and that they undergo no alteration, either in number or in size or in light or in any other respect; that they always remain the same, like unto themselves in all respects, no years wearing them away. Furthermore, the observations of all the founders of the science, made some thousands of years ago, testify that all the stars have always retained the same number, position, order, motion, and size as they are found, by careful observation on the part of those who take delight in heavenly phenomena, to preserve even in our day. Nor do we read that it was ever before noted by any one of the founders that a new star had appeared in the celestial world, except only by Hipparchus, if we are to believe Pliny. For Hipparchus, according to Pliny, (Book II of his Natural History) noticed a star different from all others previously seen, one born in his own age . . .

It is a difficult matter, and one that requires a subtle mind, to try to determine the distances of the stars from us, because they are so incredibly far removed from the earth; nor can it be done in any way more conveniently and with greater certainty than by the measure of the parallax [diurnal], if a star have one. For if a star that is near the horizon is seen in a different place than when it is at its highest point and near the vertex, it is necessarily found in some orbit with respect to which the Earth has a sensible size . . .

In order, therefore, that I might find out in this way whether this star was in the region of the Element or among the celestial orbits, and what its distance was from the Earth itself, I tried to determine whether it had a parallax, and, if so, how great a one; and this I did in the following way: I observed the distance between this star and Schedir of Cassiopeia (for the latter and the new star were both nearly on the meridian), when the star was at its nearest point to the vertex, being only 6 degrees removed from the zenith itself . . . I made the same observation when the star was farthest from the zenith and at its nearest point to the horizon, and in each case I found that the distance from the above-mentioned fixed star was exactly the same, without the variation of a minute: namely 7 degrees and 55 minutes. Then I went through the same process, making numerous observations with other stars. Whence I conclude that this new star has no diversity of aspect, even when it is near the horizon. For otherwise in its least attitude it would have been farther away from the above-mentioned star in the breast of Cassiopeia than when in its greatest altitude. Therefore, we shall find it necessary to place this star, not in the region of the Element, below the Moon, but far above, in an orbit with respect to which the Earth has no sensible size. For if it were in the highest region of the air, below the hollow region of the Lunar sphere, it would, when nearest the horizon, have produced on the circle a sensible variation of altitude from that which it held when near the vertex . . .

This new star is neither in the region of the Element, below the Moon, nor among the orbits of the seven wandering stars, but it is in the eighth sphere, among the other fixed stars, which was what we had to prove. Hence it follows that it is not some peculiar kind of comet or some other kind of fiery meteor become visible. For none of these are generated in the heavens themselves, but they are below the Moon, in the upper region of the air, as all philosophers testify; unless one would believe with Albategnius that comets are produced, not in thin air, but in the heavens. For he believes that he has observed a comet above the Moon, in the sphere of Venus. That this can be the case, is not yet clear to me. But, please God, sometime, if a comet shows itself in our age, I will investigate the truth of the matter.

Even should we assume that it can happen (which I, in company with other philosophers, can hardly admit), still it does not follow that this star is a kind of comet; first, by reason of its very form, which is the same as the form of the real stars and different from the form of all the comets hitherto seen, and then because, in such a length of time, it advances neither latitudinally nor longitudinally by any motion of its own, as comets have been observed to do. For, although these sometimes seem to remain in one place several days, still, when the observation is made carefully by exact instruments, they are seen not to keep the same position for so very long or so very exactly. I conclude, therefore, that this star is not some kind of comet or a fiery meteor, whether these be generated beneath the Moon or above the Moon, but that it is a star shining in the firmament itself—one that has never previously been seen before our time, in any age since the beginning of the world.

THE SHAPE OF NIGHT

CHET RAYMO

Chet Raymo (1936–) wrote a weekly column in the *Boston Globe* for twenty years and continues his wide-ranging contemplations on the interplay of science and the human psyche at sciencemusings.com. The author of nine books on science and nature, including *The Path: A One-Mile Walk Through the Universe* (2003), and *Walking Zero: Discovering Cosmic Space and Time Along the Prime Meridian* (2006), he has also written three novels, most famously *The Dork of Cork* (1993). This excerpt is from *The Soul of the Night: An Astronomical Pilgrimage* (1985). A collection of meditations that inspires both mind and imagination, the book ponders such phenomena as the cone of darkness that extends from a planet like a wizard's hat.

. . .

I AM A cautious pilgrim of the night, a tentative wanderer among the stars. My awareness of my home in the universe is fleeting and incomplete. Into the homeless home of the sun-faced buddha I have stepped but briefly. My quest, such as it is, is rewarded with faint lights and scrawny cries, a trait here and a trait there, a hint of the infinite and a tingle in the spine. Of "minute particulars" I will make my way. Give me, then, the moon face. Give me the blood-red face of the moon.

IN MAY of 1503, on his fourth voyage to the New World, after many trials and adventures, Christopher Columbus sailed with two ships from Panama, intending to stop at Hispaniola for refitting before returning home to Spain. Crippled by storm and riddled by worms, the little fleet was run ashore on the north coast of Jamaica. Columbus sent twelve men in canoes to seek rescue from Hispaniola, 200 miles to the east. Then, for months, he waited with the remainder of his men for rescue. To obtain food, the Spaniards bartered beads and mirrors with the local Indians. Eventually the natives grew tired of trinkets and balked at providing provisions for the stranded sailors. Columbus saw a solution to the problem. He had with him a copy of Regiomontanus' *Ephemerides,* which contained a prediction for an eclipse of the moon at moonrise on the night of February 29, 1504. Columbus called a meeting of the local chiefs and declared that if food were not forthcoming he would cause the moon to rise "inflamed with wrath." And, as he said, even as the moon rose it was the color of blood.

On the leap-year night of February 29, 1504, the moon rose just at sunset and slipped into the shadow of the Earth. Unlike other shadows, the shadow of the Earth is red. It is stained the color of blood by long-wavelength sunlight refracted by the atmosphere around the curve of the Earth. As Columbus and the Indians watched, the Earth's red-stained shadow moved across the face of the full moon and the moon was transformed from a gold doubloon to a dusky disk of crimson. I have on many occasions watched eclipses of the moon. The effect is spooky, mysterious. If I had not known about the cone of night I would have been as chastened as the Indians of Jamaica.

NIGHT HAS a shape and that shape is a cone.

In Shelley's *Prometheus Unbound* the Earth speaks this line: "I spin beneath my pyramid of night, which points into the heavens—dreaming delight." When I first read that line many years ago I was startled by the recognition of something I had possessed all along. I had studied astronomy and optics. I knew about umbras and penumbras and the way objects cast shadows in different kinds of light. In my astronomy classes, I had drawn the necessary triangles to calculate the relative sizes and distances of the sun and Earth and moon. I suppose I had *known* all along that the Earth's shadow is cone-shaped and points darkly into sunlit space. But until I read Shelley's line I had never *experienced* night as a tall pyramid of darkness receding from the globe.

Earth wears night like a wizard's cap. The wizard's cap is long and slim and points away from the sun. It is 8,000 miles in diameter at the rim, where it fits snugly on the Earth's brow. It extends to a vertex 860,000 miles from the Earth. The wizard's cap of shadow is a hundred times taller than it is wide at the base. It reaches out three times farther from the Earth than the distance to the orbit of the moon, and when the moon in its monthly circuit happens to pass through that cap of darkness, we have an eclipse of the moon.

When next I watched the moon eclipsed it was Shelley I recalled, not the astronomy text. The curved surface of the Earth's pyramidal shadow moved across the moon's full face and traced cone-shaped night. Night has not been the same since. Now night has a shape. It is the difference between *knowing* and *seeing*. There is a Zen story about a man who when he was young saw the trees as trees, the wind as wind, and the moon as the moon. As he grew older he began to ask himself why the trees grew as they did, why the winds blew from the four corners of the Earth, and why the moon waxed and waned. Everything he saw posed a question, and all of his time was spent pursuing answers. Then there came a time when the trees were again trees and the wind was again the wind and the moon was again the moon. After I read Shelley, I watched an eclipse of the moon. The moon slipped into the Earth's red shadow. For a moment the moon had the round red face of the buddha, poised in the pyramid of night. For a moment it was just the moon.

THE EARTH spins beneath its cone of night. The Earth orbits the sun, and its ruddy shadow cap goes with it, always pointing toward infinity. Under that darkling cap badgers scuttle in ditches, stalking night-crawling slugs and beetles. Bats thrash the air and squeal a high-pitched cry that only children hear.

Owls in oaks hoot at the moon. Under that darkling cap go possums, foxes, raccoons, the creatures with the big eyes, glowworms, friar's lanterns, will-o'-the-wisps. Under that darkling cap go spooks and goblins, incubi and succubi, bogeys and banshees, the Prince of Darkness. Astronomers mount their tall chairs and point their instruments into the long cap, following Earth's shadow up the Chain of Being, level by level, choir by choir, rank by rank, past the Fortunate Isles, through Elysian Fields, beyond Zion, and into the sea without shore where stars and galaxies beckon and quasars frighten like St. Elmo's fires.

Night is a cone because the Earth is round and smaller than the sun. It may have been the observation of the rounded curve of the Earth's shadow on the moon during an eclipse that led the Greeks to the astonishing discovery that the Earth is a sphere. Of course, they first had to have guessed that it was *the Earth's shadow* that caused the eclipse of the moon, rather than sky dragons or malevolent gods. The Greeks were mathematical. The Greeks replaced Baal and Zeus with Euclid. They drew circles and straight lines in the dust and saw in those constructions that the night is a cone. The straight edge and the compass were their telescope. But it took more than mathematics for the Greeks to *experience* the spherical Earth. In the end, it was *imagination* that gave the Earth its spherical shape, an act of insight as pure and focused as a circle is pure and focused, an insight that flashed straight away to the truth like a straight line. I have a friend, Mike Horne, who teaches astronomy with that kind of imagination. I have often watched him with groups of students under the stars, cavorting outrageously to convey a feeling for the Earth's

sphericity. He stretches his long arm to point to the sun somewhere over the horizon in Asia's sky. He arches his eyebrows and
stands on tiptoes to peer over the curve of the Earth for a star that
set the previous night. He moves his hands in great round circles
as if to embrace the globe. As I watch him, I find myself pushing up onto tiptoes and lifting my eyebrows, sympathetically, the
way a parent opens his mouth when feeding a child, to encompass
in my mind's eye the huge round hump of the Earth.

All of the planets wear caps of night. Every object near a star
casts a pyramidal shadow. If an astronaut floating free of Earth
orbit puts his feet toward the sun, his wizard's cap of darkness
is a hundred feet long. The moon's shadow cap, by a wonderful
coincidence, is almost exactly as long as the average distance of
the moon from the Earth. If the moon is near apogee (its greatest distance from the Earth) and passes exactly between the
Earth and the sun, the vertex of its shadow falls just short of the
surface of the Earth. In this circumstance, the sun is still visible
around the moon as a ring of brilliant light, and we have what
is called an annular (ring-shaped) eclipse of the sun. When the
moon is not near apogee its shadow reaches to the Earth, and
when the moon passes between the Earth and sun the apex of
its shadow slices into the Earth like a surgeon's knife. Those
who are lucky enough to live within the swath of that stroke
will experience one of nature's most spectacular special effects,
a total eclipse of the sun. Viewers of a total eclipse stand in the
tip of moon's night, a few moments of borrowed darkness in
daytime when bats fly, owls hoot, and badgers peek from their
burrows.

Sometimes, when the moon is just the right distance from the Earth, its shadow brushes the surface of the Earth as gently as the tip of a feather, and the eclipse of the sun is at the borderline between annular and total. The eclipse of May 30, 1984, was just such an eclipse. The moon's shadow reached to within such a narrow distance of the Earth's surface that one could almost have jumped into its vertex. The tip of the dark feather passed just above New Orleans, Atlanta, Greensboro, and Petersburg, Virginia, and moved out to sea along Maryland's eastern shore. The highest mountains of the moon's limb reached to the sun's edge and covered it. But sunlight glimmered through lunar valleys like diamonds on a necklace, like a bowl of light reduced to its broken glittering rim. In Shelley's poem, this is the full line the Earth speaks: "I spin beneath my pyramid of night, Which points into the heavens—dreaming delight, Murmuring victorious joy in my enchanted sleep; As a youth lulled in love-dreams faintly sighing, Under the shadow of his beauty lying, Which round his rest a watch of light and warmth doth keep." And the Moon responds: "As in the soft and sweet eclipse, When soul meets soul on lover's lips." On May 30, 1984, the moon interrupted the sun's watch of light and warmth with a kiss so gentle it was barely felt.

EVERY OBJECT near a star wears a cone of night. Near every star there is a ring of cone-shaped shadows that point into space like a crown of thorns. The sun's family of nights includes the shadows of nine planets, several dozen moons, and an army of asteroids. Every particle of dust in the space of the solar system casts its own tiny pyramid of darkness. The sun bristles with nights like a sea urchin prickly with shadowy spines.

Earth's cone of night is the Paraclete that brings the gift of deep space and deep time. On the planet's daylight side the atmosphere scatters sunlight into an obscuring blanket of blue, the Earth's "blue Mundane shell," William Blake called it, a "hard coating of matter that separates us from Eternity." But when we turn with the spinning Earth into night's dark cone, we glimpse the universe. Years ago I read a science fiction story about a planet in a system with four suns. Only once in 2,000 years did all four suns set at the same time and the sky go dark. When that singular event came to pass, the people of the planet saw night for the first time and were overwhelmed by its majesty.

The pyramid of night is Earth's narrow chink in its blue armor. Blake says: "If the doors of perception were cleansed, everything would appear to man as it is, infinite. For man has closed himself up, till he sees all things thro' narrow chinks of his cavern." The blue air closes us up. Only through the crack of night do we glimpse the Infinite. Only through the crack of night can we seek our sun-faced buddhas. Through that cone-shaped chink in the Earth's blue mundane shell we court Infinity the way Pyramus courted Thisbe.

THE MOONWATCHERS
OF LASCAUX

DAVID WHITEHOUSE

David Whitehouse is a British astronomer and a former science editor for the BBC. The winner of dozens of awards for television, radio, newspaper, and Web-based science reporting, Whitehouse has published two books, *The Sun: A Biography* (2004) and its companion, *The Moon: A Biography* (2001), from which this excerpt is taken. A blend of astronomy, history, and myth, the books touch on every aspect of these astronomical familiars, from how they became fixtures in our sky to how humankind has viewed them since prehistory. Still, Whitehouse cautions, "You can know all the facts about the moon, all its measurements, the chemical composition of its rocks and the ages of its surface features, but if you just know the facts, you will never know the real moon."

. . .

A FULL MOON rose into a cloudless Dordogne sky that September evening. Twenty thousand years ago this place was a small temperate oasis on the southern edge of the great Würm glacier. The ice age that had gripped Europe would continue to hold it for many thousands of years yet. Ancient man made his home here and left behind something extraordinary. As we sped along deserted country lanes, through darkening forests of oak and chestnut, the moon peered over the limestone cliffs that seem to be everywhere littered with evidence of the Cro-Magnon. Soon, across the valley, we saw what we were headed for. "There," said my guide, pointing at it, "there is the Hill of Lascaux."

The moon still played between the trees as we made our way to the entrance of the cave. As I descended the steps I noticed the sudden drop in temperature, as if signifying the portal to another world, another time. Above ground it was a warm, balmy autumnal night, considerably more pleasant than the damp and misty England I had left earlier that day. It took a few moments for my eyes to become adapted to the cave's half-light. I had heard about this place of course and seen the pictures of it but as I entered the "Hall of the Bulls" I knew instantly that nothing could have prepared me for its powerful, overwhelming beauty. Outlined in black and coloured with vivid brown, ochre and rusty-red, bulls and antelope were stampeding across the walls. They seemed to be converging on some significant point in the cave with their movement captured so well that I would not have been surprised to see them move. The prehistoric cave paintings of Lascaux are surely one of the greatest artistic achievements of my species.

I was here with Dr. Michael Rappenglueck of Munich

University, a man who has studied these caves, and many others, and has begun to uncover some of their mysteries.

Above the shoulder of one magnificent bull there was a collection of small dots. Their familiar shape meant that Dr. Rappenglueck did not have to convince me that they were the Pleiades (or the "Seven Sisters"). To me it is staggering that the constellation of Taurus the Bull is so ancient that it stretches back over 15,000 years to the time these caves were painted. These people looked up at the same stars that we see today and bequeathed us a bull with a tiny cluster of stars on its shoulder. I will never look at Taurus the same way again. But there was more.

To one side of the main chamber was the co-called "Shaft of the Dead Man." If you look at it the right way you can see the three bright stars that are known today as the "Summer Triangle." This is by far the world's oldest star map but not a star map as we know it. Some stars are there but this prehistoric cosmos was also full of animals and spirit-guides.

The moon was here as well.

Back to the main chamber and down slightly to the entrance of a spectacular passageway adorned with bulls and horses and strange symbols. "Look here," said Dr. Rappenglueck pointing up at the ceiling.

Beneath a horse so lifelike that you just know these people loved their animals, I could see a row of dots, some of them forming a loop. This is believed to show the moon going through its monthly cycle. It is the oldest lunar calendar yet discovered. I pointed to the loop looking puzzled. "Perhaps a representation of the brightness of the full moon," he speculated.

Another group of dots may also be connected with the moon. "It shows half of the moon's monthly cycle," Dr. Rappenglueck said. "At the new moon, when it vanishes from the sky, they have painted an empty square, perhaps symbolically representing the absent moon."

"Did you know," said my guide glancing around, "in many ancient cultures, such as Assyria's, a bull represents the moon god? I suspect the antlers of these bulls may be also symbolically representing the moon, as they did ten thousand years later in ancient Egypt."

We left the cave with a sense of loss. You felt you wanted to get to know these people. That they would be waiting at the entrance uttering strange words with their flat stone lamps that burned animal fat just extinguished, their hands still covered in ochre and black pigment. I almost felt that the answers to my questions would be just a few steps away and that the outside world had changed. But the moon was a little higher as we made our way back through the still and silent trees. I felt that in a way I had become one of them, one of the moonwatchers of Lascaux.

NOCTURNE

———

WAYNE GRADY

Wayne Grady (1948–) is the author of nine books of essays and narrative nonfiction as well as a noted anthologist and translator. He has travelled with scientific expeditions to the Gobi Desert, the North Pole, and Patagonia, writing about the natural world and the place of humans in it. Two-time winner of the Science in Society Book Award for *The Quiet Limit of the World: A Journey to the North Pole to Investigate Global Warming* (1997) and *Tree: A Life Story* (with David Suzuki, 2004), Grady writes about the night in *Bringing Back the Dodo: Lessons in Natural and Unnatural History* (2006). In this excerpt, he explores how the forces of evolution and extinction have shaped the living world and, in particular, our ability to see in the dark.

. . .

HANGING IN THE National Gallery in Ottawa is a painting by William Kurelek that looks, from a distance, like a large square canvas painted black. Upon closer inspection, it is a night scene.

In the centre is a large, ploughed field, and to the right, a water-filled ditch running down the side, with a footbridge crossing it. You can just discern a group of people on the bridge, rushing across, seemingly panic-stricken (one man has lost his footing and is falling into the ditch). It seems to be a religious gathering, all are carrying copies of *The Watchtower*, and they are looking over their shoulders at something that is happening in the field, something terrifying. When you follow their gaze you see it is an owl, white, spectral, its eyes and claws wide open, plunging down through the darkness toward a family of tiny, white mice. The mice, too, have seen the owl, and are scampering off to the left, as panicky as the people on the bridge. The painting is enti-tled, "Blind Leading the Blind."

Carl Jung believed that when an artist is fully engaged in his or her work, he or she is tapping into some kind of collec-tive subconscious, and when a viewer sees and responds to that work, he or she is drawing from that same subconscious source. So, what is going on in this painting? It is night. There are two groups, the humans and the mice. The mice are frightened, but so are the humans. The mice have good reason to be fright-ened—they are about to be dive-bombed by an owl (although in life mice probably never see the owl that gets them). But why are the people also terrified? They are in no danger, except that created by their own panic. And if both groups are blind, who is leading whom?

It must be the night itself that has frightened the people, a night filled with unseen, or unseeable, terrors. Hence, probably, the religious motif. Night and religion are commonly linked in Western art. Christopher Dewdney, in his book *Acquainted With the Night,* notes that one of the earliest paintings of a night scene is an Egyptian image of the sky goddess Nut arched over the earth, who is both her brother and lover. Night is the time of spectral beings. It is no accident that Hamlet's fateful encounter with his father's ghost takes place at midnight. "I am thy father's spirit," says the Ghost, "doomed for a certain term to walk the night." There is no logical reason why ghosts should be more active after sundown than before it, but Shakespeare, who knew a nighthawk from a handsaw when he saw one ("handsaw," by the way, is a corruption of "herronsew," an old name for a juvenile heron), also knew how to evoke the classic involuntary fright responses from his spectators: goose flesh, widening of the eyes, stiffening of the neck hairs (or, as Shakespeare himself more eloquently put it, scenes that would "freeze thy young blood, Make thy two eyes, like stars, start from their spheres . . . And each particular hair to stand on end, Like quills upon the fretful porpentine"). Setting the scene at night, as directors of modern horror films instinctively know, is guaranteed to make the audience squirm in their seats. "'Tis now the very witching time of night," Hamlet says, "When Churchyards yawn and Hell itself breathes out Contagion to this world."

Witches, like ghosts, could (and did) just as easily practise their black arts during the day, so why do we have them cavorting by candlelight? It may be because early sorceresses achieved their ecstatic visions by dosing themselves with the juice of the night-blooming plant *Datura stramonium,* a fragrant, hallucinogenic member of the nightshade family, known to Thoreau as thorn-apple or Devil's trumpet, from the shape of its flowers. Datura contains a number of mind-altering compounds, including hyoscyamine, atropine, and scopolamine, "a tropane alkaloid," writes Wade Davis in *One River*. "If you take a big whack, it brings on a wild, crazed state, total disorientation, delirium, foaming at the mouth, a wicked thirst, terrifying visions that fuse into a dreamless sleep, followed by complete amnesia." Did the Pilgrim Fathers check Salem's gardens for datura? The plant was found growing wild in Virginia in 1676 by a group of British soldiers on their way to put down the Bacon Rebellion; they boiled and ate it as a salad (the British boil everything, even their salads). "The effect," according to the eighteenth-century historian Robert Beverley, who must have disliked British soldiers, "was a very pleasant comedy."

But the real reason we fill the night with terrors may have more to do with our natural history than with religion. The question is: what put those terrifying images in our subconscious in the first place? Kurelek's haunting painting provides, I think, a tanatalizing clue. The only blind beings at night are us. Mice can see in the dark as well as owls can hear. We can do neither very effectively. We haven't always been that way; far back in the evolutionary history of our species, we were nocturnal creatures. When we emerged from the night, we traded in night vision for colour vision, and darkness has frightened us ever since.

AS MAMMALS, we are descended from an extinct group of reptiles, the therapsids, that crawled the Earth some 400 million years ago. They were the planet's dominant vertebrate life form until dinosaurs took over about 250 million years ago. Triassic dinosaurs were large and cold-blooded and therefore diurnal—they couldn't maintain their body temperature if they moved around much during the night—so as the dinosaurs seized the day, some of the smaller therapsids survived by becoming nocturnal: in paleoeconomic parlance, the night was empty, and the therapsids colonized it. To do so, they had to develop higher body temperatures, which they eventually maintained by becoming warm-blooded and developing hair, and they augmented their reduced eyesight with acute senses of smell and hearing. Sometime in the late Triassic or early Jurassic, some of them became mammals.

Most present-day mammals—like the mice in Kurelek's painting—are still nocturnal, while most reptiles, as well as birds (except for Kurelek's owl), remain diurnal. The big exception among mammals is us, the primates. Prosimians broke off from the main mammalian line about 60 million years ago, shortly after that famous meteorite smacked down in Yucatán and rid the planet of dinosaurs. For some reason—perhaps because the day suddenly became empty, whereas the night had become full of a wide range of competing (or frightening) predators—the primates returned to daytime activity; they became diurnal, and the night became a distant, disturbing memory, a bad dream. One of the ways they were able to do this was by developing a new kind of eye.

The evolution of the eye is a logician's nightmare, full of twists and unknown turns and even, it seems, at least one impossibility. Darwin worried that anti-evolutionists would seize upon the eye to challenge his theory of natural selection: how, he imagined his detractors demanding to know, could such a miraculous organ as the eye have simply developed, stage by stage, from nothing? Surely it had to have been created by God. "If it could be demonstrated that any complex organ existed which could not possibly have been formed by numerous, successive, slight modifications," he wrote in *The Origin of Species*, "my theory would absolutely break down." Anything that apparently leapt into existence without a slew of previous forms preserved in the fossil record could be seized upon to discredit his theory of how evolution works.

His problem, of course, was the complete absence of fossil evidence for any organ's gradual development. Bones and teeth fossilize, and skin and feathers have left impressions in volcanic dust, and so a succession of subtle changes in them can be traced. But soft organs almost never become fossils. There are no dinosaur hearts or lungs to study, alas. (Certainly in Darwin's day nothing of the kind existed; in the past few decades dinosaurs with fossilized skin have been found, and I have seen a Carnatosaur specimen in Argentina with skin-covered muscles, but no eyeballs.) Darwin had to posit the evolution of the eyeball, which began as a cluster of primitive, photosensitive nerves "surrounded by pigment-cells and covered by translucent skin, but without any lens or other refractive body," serving merely to distinguish light from darkness. Step by infinitesimal step, over eons of time, the cluster evolved "into a structure even as perfect as an eagle's eye."

The resultant eyeball is little more than a hollow sack (the sclera) surrounding a photosensitive liner (the retina). The retina is essentially an extension of ganglia from the brain attached to a layer of cells of two types: rods and cones. Photons of light enter the hollow eyeball through a lens fitted into the cornea, are absorbed by the rods and cones arranged along the back wall, and are changed into electrical impulses that pass along the ganglia to the brain, which reinterprets the impulses back into an image.

That sounds simple enough. Digital cameras work much the same way when hooked up to a computer. But this is where it starts to get unpredictable (i.e., human). The rods deal with black and white; the cones with colour. Because the eye is thought to have evolved from cells whose sole function was to distinguish dark from light, thus triggering certain hormonal secretions, you'd think the rods would have come first, with the cones coming along later as the eye evolved to perform more complex tasks. But not so: the cones came first. Those sluggish therapsids could discern colours, maybe more of them than we can. They lost much of that ability when they became nocturnal: they didn't need colour vision any more, because they couldn't see colour at night anyway. That's when the number of cones dwindled and were outnumbered by rods.

Most modern mammals still have more rods than cones; they can see black and white and all the shades of grey, but the only colours they perceive are those on the low-wavelength end of the spectrum: blue and green. They are dichromatic. They cannot distinguish red from green. Despite all the hoopla, matadors might just as well be waving a lime-green pillowcase in front of a bull as a fiery red cape. It's all the same to the bull: it's the indignity that infuriates him, not the colour red. Similarly, to a cat, a canary could be white or magenta or puce; cats can only distinguish green from blue. They aren't biologically inclined to hunt birds anyway, given that birds are diurnal and cats nocturnal. Cats are meant to hunt rodents and other small mammals, not birds . . .

Primates are the anomaly. When prosimians broke off from the main mammalian line by becoming diurnal, they evolved an extra set of colour-detecting cones in their retinae. Re-evolving a character that has evolved out is supposed to be an evolutionary impossibility. Dollo's Law on the irreversibility of evolution (Louis Dollo was a Belgian paleontologist who was the first to realize that some of the bigger dinosaurs were bipedal, thus providing an early link between dinosaurs and birds) has it that once a feature, like gills or quadrupedality, has evolved out, it's gone forever. According to Dollo, flightless birds like the ostrich and the rhea (assuming that they were once flighted and have since lost that ability) will never fly again.

But somehow, Dollo's Law notwithstanding, when the prosimians split away from dichromatic mammals, they re-evolved cone dominance, thus becoming trichromatic primates, which is why we can see high-wavelength reds and yellows (a range that allows us to see 2.3 million different colours). It is unDarwinian to ponder the reasons for this evolutionary about-face—evolution doesn't have a reason, it just happens and species take advantage of it . . .

IT IS our eyes that made us successful day creatures. But they also robbed us of the night. When we emerged from nocturnality to become diurnal, is it possible that we retained, embedded somewhere deep in our subconscious, the memory of a darkness filled with predators, a night realm we could no longer see, but which we knew to be rife with danger? An ache that religion salved? Freud believed that we invest our nighttime dreams with images gathered during the daytime: "day residues," he called them. Could our new, daytime imaginings be fuelled by a species memory of our nocturnal selves, filled with "night residues"? If so, it might explain why so many of the stories we scare ourselves with take place at night, and contain creatures we cannot ordinarily see. Witches and ghosts, ogres, transgenetic beasts. Such creatures are our night residues.

One of my favourite poems is John Donne's "Nocturnal Upon St. Lucy's Day." Saint Lucy's Day, by the old Elizabethan reckoning, was December 21 (it is now the thirteenth), the winter solstice, the shortest day of the year and therefore the longest night. In his poem, Donne calls it "the year's midnight." It is a singularly dark and melancholic poem. When Donne decides to be gloomy, he can be downright suicidal: "The world's whole sap is sunk," he writes. "For I am every dead thing . . . the grave / Of all, that's nothing." He never tells us why he is so despondent, although he hints at the death of love. Has his lover died? Has she left him? Or is it all love that is dead, impossible, always tantalizingly out of reach? Whatever is afflicting him, it is definitely something more than an early case of Seasonal Affective Disorder. Like the distant sun, he is "re-begot / Of absence, darkness, death—things which are not."

Or things which are no longer, perhaps. In fixing his despair on that particular day, he hit upon the ideal symbol, one that suggests his poetic imagination went fishing in the Jungian pool and pulled up something from our evolutionary past. St. Lucy is the patron saint of those afflicted in the eyes, especially of the blind. She lived in Syracuse, Sicily, in the fourth century. In one version of her story, when a nobleman fell in love with her because, he claimed, of the beauty of her eyes, she plucked them out, Oedipus-like, and gave them to him on a platter. "Now let me live to God," she said, and he apparently did. In Christian art she is represented with a palm leaf in one hand and in the other a platter, on which roll two sightless orbs. Like loveless Donne, and like all of us at one time in our evolutionary history, she dwelled in perpetual night.

NIGHT FISHING

SPARSE GREY HACKLE

Sparse Grey Hackle was the pen name of Alfred Waterbury Miller (1892–1983), a Wall Street reporter obsessed with fly-fishing. Through the thirties and forties, he fished Catskill streams for trout, becoming the confidant of a dying generation of fishermen. When Miller noticed the streams becoming polluted, he wrote irate articles to local newspapers under the name Sparse Grey Hackle. The moniker continued to show up in outdoor sporting magazines, and eventually his essays were collected in a private publication from the Anglers' Club of New York (Miller edited their *Bulletin*). Published by Crown Publishers as *Fishless Days, Angling Nights* (1971), the stories have made Sparse Grey Hackle an icon among fly fishermen. "Night Fishing," excerpted here, is considered by many to be the finest work on fishing ever published in America.

.   .   .

HEAT AND FEAR oppressed the land, for it was one of those stifling, humid August nights when the whole countryside is awake and every living thing is abroad on the business of life and death. The darkness was so thick and close that one tried instinctively to push it aside, and the air was heavy with the menace of predators and the terror of their prey. The river was soundless save for a faint spattering at my feet, a mere whisper which I could not identify until I turned on my little flashlight and discovered in the very margin of the stream, where it feathered off to nothing on a sandy beach, a dark line of what appeared to be stranded twigs and chaff. It was a horde of the tiniest of minnows, which had taken refuge in the ultimate edge of water and still leaped frantically over each other in their efforts to be farthest from the prowling fish they knew would soon be seeking them.

I waded across the broad river to where a little cold feeder entered it and began to cast a big wet fly on a heavy leader, for this is the season when the hellgrammites rise from the river bottom and swim ashore to pupate under stones before hatching into huge nocturnal dobson flies. It was too early yet for big fish to be feeding, but there might be a stray around, and anyway, I wanted to be fishing. So for a couple of hours I inched along silently on felt-shod feet working my fly in the cooler water along the bank, where a fish might be harboring. At midnight it was still hot and breathless. Perspiration dripped off my face, and inside my high waders I was soaked with it. I was weary of swinging the big ten-foot fly rod, too, so I went ashore and sat down for a while before I made my way up to the head of the long pool.

The sky had somehow brightened now, and the darkness, so thick and close before, appeared thin and luminous. It seemed as if I could see farther than I really could, but at least I could make out the stranded log on the far bank shining white as bone. I replaced my wet fly with a deer-hair bug to imitate some blundering moth and began to work out line along the far side of the river. It is difficult to get out in darkness just the length needed to reach one's target but not impossible if one is familiar with the water and his rod, so when I picked up the cast and pushed it straight across at the log, I was confident that my bug would drop right in front of it.

I brought my hand down hard and the bug smacked the water. A white flower of foam blossomed in front of the log, and blossomed again when I swept the tip back in a hard strike. I was into a fish! It headed down the current, and I held the rod high overhead and reeled desperately to take up the slack. I seemed to be choking, and it took me a moment to discover that it was because I was holding my breath.

Alas, the fish was strong but not strong enough; fighting but not fighting hard. Suspicion at once changed to conviction, and conviction became certainty when I brought the fish into the circle of strange pale light cast by the little flashlight which by now I held between my teeth. It was a chub—an alderman, the grandfather of all the chub in the river, a chub as round as a rolling pin, one with pretensions to rise above his class and act like a trout, but still . . . a chub.

I unhooked and returned him—gently, because I was grateful to him for providing a little action; stowed away my flashlight and felt for my pipe. Only then did I realize that my heart was pounding slowly and heavily, like a burned-out main bearing.

That is night fishing, the essence of angling, the emperor of all sports. It is a gorgeous gambling game in which one stakes the certainty of long hours of faceless fumbling, nerve-wracking starts, frights, falls, and fishless baskets against the off-chance of hooking into—not landing necessarily or even probably, but hooking into—a fish as long and heavy as a railroad tie and as unmanageable as a runaway submarine. It combines the wary stalking and immobile patience of an Indian hunter with sudden, violent action, the mystery and thrill of the unknown, a stimulating sense of isolation and self-reliance, and an unparalleled opportunity to be close to nature since most creatures are really nocturnal in habit.

Above all, it provides the stimulation of sudden fright at the startling things which continually occur in the dark, and in fact I incline to believe that that is the greatest lure of the sport. In all of the night-fishing experiences that I recall, the outstanding thing was always that I was scared half to death . . .

It was in early May on the Beaverkill and I had not found fish, so, misled by the warm sun and balmy air, I thought there might be night fishing in my favorite pool, the Wagon Tracks. Normally Cairns' Ford, at the head of the pool, is almost out of the water except for a little channel close to the road side of the stream, but now I found it knee-deep all the way across, pants-pocket deep in the channel and of course running like a milltail. It was a tough crossing in daylight; I did not stop to think what it would be like at night.

I found that what was normally the shallow side of the pool had been scoured by floods, and in the high water I had to wade close to the bank. It was not a good sort of night water in that condition, but I was still bemused, so I put on a big stonefly nymph and started working down, casting straight across and letting the fly swing round, then fishing it back close to the bank, an inch at a time. I worked along on numbing legs for hours, staring blankly into darkness relieved only when a car passed along the road on the other side. The water was quiet, dead in fact; and then I thought I felt a light touch on the nymph right below me, just as it would be finishing its swing. Action at last! Surely something had lipped the nymph; that was just the right point in its swing to expect it. Could I make the fish come again?

Reeling up the slack I had already worked in so that my next cast would come to exactly the same length, I chucked the nymph across the current again, and as it began to swing I unconsciously leaned forward with my arms extended in an attitude of hair-trigger alertness. The line straightened and I knew the big nymph swinging behind it was approaching the spot. Now . . .

Something, a mink perhaps, leaped off the bank and struck the water right under my outstretched arms; as it hit, a good-sized fish leaped out and made its escape.

I stood fixed; I couldn't have moved to save my life. The sweet, sickening taste which is the real flavor of fear filled my mouth and my heart hammered in my throat. I began to strangle and knew I was holding my breath, but I could not command my lungs to function.

When I had recovered the power of movement I decided that I was through, took down my rod and got my little flashlight out to go back across the ford. Now the ford ran at a diagonal and my target was a clump of bushes on the other bank. I couldn't see the bushes with my little light, but I could see the stream bottom—the shallow ford and the deeper water on either side of it. So I went along all right for perhaps a quarter of the way, and then my flashlight played out.

I had only a couple of hundred feet to go, more or less, but that is a long distance when the water is too high, the night too dark and the way too uncertain. I worked ahead feeling for the shallower water but soon got into the position familiar to every night fisherman in which one seems to be surrounded by deeper water. All right; I would stand still until a car came along to shine its headlights on my brushy marker. But this was wartime, with gasoline rationing in force, and people were not driving much at night. I think only the fact that it was Saturday night, traditional "night out" for countrymen as well as city folk, saved me.

I stood there a while beside that short, ugly rapid roaring down into deep water, remembering that I couldn't swim even without high waders and heavy hobnailed shoes to handicap me. Then a car flashed by and I found my marker and stepped out boldly until once more I seemed to be hemmed in by deep water. As I recall, I had to wait for four cars in order to reach the edge of the deeper channel, ten feet from the bank.

I stepped down into it cautiously with one foot, found a rolling stone, dislodged it, and got solid footing; I brought the other foot forward, worked it in and out of some sharp-angled pockets, and planted it beside the first. The water was halfway above my knees now, tearing at my legs, growling and foaming. The steep pounding rapid was white in the darkness and what I could see looked as bad as it sounded. I shuffled a foot forward, then brought the other one up beside it; the water was an inch deeper. I felt and withdrew with first one foot and then the other, then inched half a step downstream to get around something high and slippery. I completed another shuffling step. At last I was just two steps from safety, one into deeper water and the next up onto the bank. I put the rod joints in my mouth to have both hands free and resolved to throw myself forward and grab for bushes if I felt myself going. I took a deep breath and stepped out, and as so often happens, anticipation was worse than reality. My foot held, and in the next instant I was hauling myself out.

I sat down on the running board of my car, filled my pipe, and looked at my watch. It was 1:00 AM daylight saving time. My feet were numb, my legs ached, and my mouth was dry, and when I took off my waders I discovered that my knees were trembling slightly but steadily and uncontrollably. Fatigue? Not on your life. I was scared stiff.

THE ALLIGATORS
OF LAKE DEXTER

WILLIAM BARTRAM

William Bartram (1739–1823) was the son of John Bartram, America's first acknowledged botanist. From a young age, he worked in his father's botanical garden and accompanied him on botanizing expeditions, honing his talent for accurate and elegant drawings of flora in the wild. In 1773, he embarked on his own plant-collecting journey through the American Southeast, and eighteen years later, he published an account of the expedition, *Travels through North and South Carolina, Georgia, East and West Florida* (1791), which includes this episode of night terror in the Everglades. Inspired in its observations, evocative in its prose, the book was lauded as a work of literature as well as a benchmark of American nature writing. Widely read in both Europe and North America, it influenced such Romantic writers as Wordsworth and Coleridge.

. . .

EVENING NOW DRAWING on, I was anxious to reach some high bank of the river, where I intended to lodge; and agreeably to my wishes, I soon after discovered, on the west shore, a little promontory, at the turning of the river, contracting it here to about one hundred and fifty yards in width. This promontory is a peninsula, containing about three acres of high ground, and is one entire orange grove, with a few live oaks, magnolias and palms. Upon doubling the point, I arrived at the landing, which is a circular harbour, at the foot of the bluff, the top of which is about twelve feet high; and back of it is a large cypress swamp, that spreads each way, the right wing forming the west coast of the little lake, and the left stretching up the river many miles, and encompassing a vast space of low grassy marshes. From this promontory, looking eastward across the river, I beheld a landscape of low country, unparalleled as I think; on the left is the east coast of the little lake, which I had just passed; and from the orange bluff at the lower end, the high forests begin, and increase in breadth from the shore of the lake, making a circular sweep to the right, and contain many hundred thousand acres of meadow; and this grand sweep of high forests encircles, as I apprehend, at least twenty miles of these green fields, interspersed with hommocks or islets of evergreen trees, where the sovereign magnolia and lordly palm stand conspicuous. The islets are high shelly knolls, on the sides of creeks or branches of the river, which wind about and drain off the superabundant waters that cover these meadows during the winter season.

The evening was temperately cool and calm. The crocodiles began to roar and appear in uncommon numbers along the shores and in the river. I fixed my camp in an open plain, near

the utmost projection of the promontory, under the shelter of a
large live oak, which stood on the highest part of the ground
and but a few yards from my boat. From this open, high situation, I had a free prospect of the river, which was a matter of
no trivial consideration to me, having good reason to dread the
subtle attacks of the alligators, who were crowding about my
harbour. Having collected a good quantity of wood for the purpose of keeping up a light and smoke during the night, I began
to think of preparing my supper, when, upon examining my
stores, I found but a scanty provision. I thereupon determined,
as the most expeditious way of supplying my necessities, to
take my bob and try for some trout. About one hundred yards
above my harbour began a cove or bay of the river, out of which
opened a large lagoon. The mouth or entrance from the river
to it was narrow, but the waters soon after spread and formed a
little lake, extending into the marshes, its entrance and shores
within I observed to be verged with floating lawns of the pistia
and nymphea and other aquatic plants; these I knew were excel-
lent haunts for trout.

The verges and islets of the lagoon were elegantly embel-
lished with flowering plants and shrubs; the laughing coots
with wings half spread were tripping over the little coves and
hiding themselves in the tufts of grass; young broods of the
painted summer teal, skimming the still surface of the waters,
and following the watchful parent unconscious of danger, were
frequently surprised by the voracious trout; and he, in turn, as
often by the subtle greedy alligator. Behold him rushing forth

from the flags and reeds. His enormous body swells. His plaited tail brandished high, floats upon the lake. The waters like a cataract descend from his opening jaws. Clouds of smoke issue from his dilated nostrils. The earth trembles with his thunder. When immediately from the opposite coast of the lagoon, emerges from the deep his rival champion. They suddenly dart upon each other. The boiling surface of the lake marks their rapid course, and a terrific conflict commences. They now sink to the bottom folded together in horrid wreaths. The water becomes thick and discoloured. Again they rise, their jaws clap together, re-echoing through the deep surrounding forests. Again they sink, when the contest ends at the muddy bottom of the lake, and the vanquished makes a hazardous escape, hiding himself in the muddy turbulent waters and sedge on a distant shore. The proud victor exulting returns to the place of action. The shores and forests resound his dreadful roar, together with the triumphing shouts of the plaited tribes around, witnesses of the horrid combat.

My apprehensions were highly alarmed after being a spectator of so dreadful a battle. It was obvious that every delay would but tend to increase my dangers and difficulties, as the sun was near setting, and the alligators gathered around my harbour from all quarters. From these considerations I concluded to be expeditious in my trip to the lagoon, in order to take some fish. Not thinking it prudent to take my fusée with me, lest I might lose it overboard in case of a battle, which I had every reason to dread before my return, I therefore furnished myself with a club for my defence, went on board, and penetrating the first line of those which surrounded my harbour, they gave way; but being pursued by several very large ones, I kept strictly on the watch, and paddled with all my might towards the entrance of the lagoon, hoping to be sheltered there from the multitude of my assailants; but ere I had half-way reached the place, I was attacked on all sides, several endeavouring to overset the canoe. My situation now became precarious to the last degree: two very large ones attacked me closely, at the same instant, rushing up with their heads and part of their bodies above the water, roaring terribly and belching floods of water over me. They struck their jaws together so close to my ears, as almost to stun me, and I expected every moment to be dragged out of the boat and instantly devoured, but I applied my weapons so effectually about me, though at random, that I was so successful as to beat them off a little; when, finding that they designed to renew the battle, I made for the shore, as the only means left me for my preservation, for, by keeping close to it, I should have my enemies on one side of me only, whereas I was before surrounded by them, and there was a probability, if pushed to the last extremity, of saving myself, by jumping out of the canoe on shore, as it is easy to outwalk them on land, although comparatively as swift as lightning in the water...

Returning to my camp I found it undisturbed, and then continued on to the extreme point of the promontory, where I saw a scene, new and surprising, which at first threw my senses into such a tumult, that it was some time before I could comprehend what was the matter; however, I soon accounted for the prodigious assemblage of crocodiles at this place, which exceeded every thing of the kind I had ever heard of.

How shall I express myself so as to convey an adequate idea of it to the reader, and at the same time avoid raising suspicions of my want of veracity? Should I say, that the river (in this place) from shore to shore, and perhaps near half a mile above and below me, appeared to be one solid bank of fish, of various kinds, pushing through this narrow pass of St. Juan's into the little lake, on their return down the river, and that the alligators were in such incredible numbers, and so close together from shore to shore, that it would have been easy to have walked across on their heads, had the animals been harmless? What expressions can sufficiently declare the shocking scene that for some minutes continued, whilst this mighty army of fish were forcing the pass? During this attempt, thousands, I may say hundreds of thousands, of them were caught and swallowed by the devouring alligators. I have seen an alligator take up out of the water several great fish at a time, and just squeeze them betwixt his jaws, while the tails of the great trout flapped about his eyes and lips, ere he had swallowed them. The horrid noise of their closing jaws, their plunging amidst the broken banks of fish, and rising with their prey some feet upright above the water, the floods of water and blood rushing out of their mouths, and the clouds of vapour issuing from their wide nostrils, were truly frightful. This scene continued at intervals during the night, as the fish came to the pass. After this sight, shocking and tremendous as it was, I found myself somewhat easier and more reconciled to my situation; being convinced that their extraordinary assemblage here was owing to this annual feast of fish; and that they were so well employed in their own element, that I had little occasion to fear their paying me a visit . . .

The noise of the crocodiles kept me awake the greater part of the night; but when I arose in the morning, contrary to my expectations, there was perfect peace; very few of them to be seen, and those were asleep on the shore. Yet I was not able to suppress my fears and apprehensions of being attacked by them in future; and indeed yesterday's combat with them, notwithstanding I came off in a manner victorious, or at least made a safe retreat, had left sufficient impression on my mind to damp my courage; and it seemed too much for one of my strength, being alone in a very small boat, to encounter such collected danger.

NIGHT ON THE GREAT BEACH

HENRY BESTON

Henry Beston (1888–1968) wrote children's books and two memoirs of his experience in the First World War before retreating, at thirty-eight, to a cabin on the far reaches of Cape Cod, Maine, to recover his war-torn soul. He stayed for two years, recording his impressions in a journal that became *The Outermost House* (1928), excerpted here. Although he continued to publish, this work became a classic. In 1964, the house was declared a National Literary Landmark; fourteen years later, it was swept away in a massive storm, leaving only the stretch of beach where Beston had often walked at night. Remembered as one of the fathers of the modern environmental movement, Beston was a thoughtful man of keen perception. "Poetry," he wrote, "is as necessary to comprehension as science."

. . .

ON THE NIGHT I write of, the first quarter of the moon hung in the west, and its light on the sheets of incoming tide coursing thin across the bar was very beautiful to see. Just after sundown

I walked to Nauset with friends who had been with me during the afternoon; the tide was still rising, and a current running in the pools. I lingered at the station with my friends till the last of sunset had died, and the light upon the planet, which had been moonlight mingled with sunset pink, had cleared to pure cold moon.

Southward, then, I turned, and because the flooded runnels were deep close by the station, I could not cross them and had to walk their inner shores. The tide had fallen half a foot, perhaps, but the breakers were still leaping up against the bar as against a wall, the greater ones still spilling over sheets of vanishing foam.

It grew darker with the westing of the moon. There was light on the western tops of the dunes, a fainter light on the lower beach and the breakers; the face of the dunes was a unity of dusk.

The tide had ebbed in the pools, and their edges were wet and dark. There was a strange contrast between the still levels of the pool and the seethe of the sea. I kept close to the land edge of the lagoons, and as I advanced my boots kicked wet spatters of sand ahead as they might have kicked particles of snow. Every spatter was a crumb of phosphorescence; I walked in a dust of stars. Behind me, in my footprints, luminous patches burned. With the double-ebb moonlight and tide, the deepening brims of the pools took shape in smouldering, wet fire. So strangely did the luminous speckles smoulder and die and glow that it seemed as if some wind were passing, by whose breath they were kindled and extinguished. Occasional whole breakers of phosphorescence rolled in out of the vague sea—the whole wave one ghostly motion, one creamy light—and, breaking against the bar, flung up pale sprays of fire.

A strange thing happens here during these luminous tides. The phosphorescence is itself a mass of life, sometimes protozoan in its origin, sometimes bacterial, the phosphorescence I write of being probably the latter. Once this living light has seeped into the beach, colonies of it speedily invade the tissues of the ten thousand thousand sand fleas which are forever hopping on this edge of ocean. Within an hour the grey bodies of these swarming amphipods, these useful, ever hungry sea scavengers *(Orchestia agilis; Talorchestia megalophthalma),* show phosphorescent pinpoints, and these points grow and unite till the whole creature is luminous. The attack is really a disease, an infection of light. The process had already begun when I arrived on the beach on the night of which I am writing, and the luminous fleas, hopping off before my boots were an extraordinary sight. It was curious to see them hop from the pool rims to the upper beach, paling as they reached the width of peaceful moonlight lying landward of the strange, crawling beauty of the pool. This infection kills them, I think; at least, I have often found the larger creature lying dead on the fringe of the beach, his huge porcelain eyes and water-grey body one core of living fire. Round and about him, disregarding, ten thousand kinsmen, carrying on life and the plan of life, ate of the bounty of the tide.

IN A MIDNIGHT LANE

LOREN EISELEY

When Loren Eiseley (1907–1977) was three, his father pointed out Halley's Comet blazing across the night sky and told him to watch for its return in seventy-five years. Eiseley didn't live long enough to see it again, but he spent his life looking at the sky, at the earth, and at every living thing that crossed his path and writing about them in eighteen books of essays, poetry, and general science, including *The Unexpected Universe* (1969). Trained as an anthropologist, his writing combines scientific exploration with a lyrical humanism and realistic optimism. This selection is from *The Night Country* (1971), a meditative memoir of his experiences as a sometime fossil hunter. Effectively probing both interior and exterior darkness, Eiseley's work is drawn from what he called "the wilderness of a single life."

. . .

SOMETIMES IN A country lane at midnight you can sense their eyes upon you—the eyes that by daylight may be the vacuous protuberant orbs of grazing cattle or the good brown eyes of farm dogs. But there, in the midnight lane, they draw off from you or silently watch you pass from their hidden coverts in the hedgerows. They are back in a secret world from which man has been shut out, and they want no truck with him after nightfall. Perhaps it is because of this that more and more we employ machines with lights and great noise to rush by these watchful shadows. My experience, therefore, may be among the last to be reported from that night world, which, with our machines to face, is slowly ebbing back into little patches of wilderness behind lighted signboards. It concerns a journey. I will not say where the journey began, but it took place in the years that have come to be called the Great Depression and was made alone and on foot. Finally I had come to a place where, far off over an endless blue plain, I could see the snow on the crests of the mountains. The city to which I was journeying lay, I knew, at the foot of the highest peak. I would keep the mountains in sight, I thought to myself, and find my own path to the city.

I climbed over a barbed-wire fence and marched directly toward the city through the blue air under the great white peak. I think sometimes now, long afterward, that it was the happiest, most independent day of my entire life. No one waited for me anywhere. I was complete in myself like a young migrating animal whose world exists totally in the present moment. The range with its drifting cattle and an occasional passing bird began to unroll beneath my stride. I meant to be across that range and over an escarpment of stone to the city at the mountain's foot before the dawn of another morning. During the entire walk I was never to meet another human being. The lights and showers shone upon or darkened my face alternately, but I was destined to share the experience with no one.

In the later afternoon, after descending into innumerable arroyos and scrambling with difficulty up the opposite side, I began to grow tired. Coming out finally into a country that was less trenched and eroded, I was trudging steadily onward when I came upon a pond. At least for all purposes it could answer to the name, though it was only a few inches deep—mere standing rainwater caught in a depression of impermeable soil and interspersed with tufts of brown buffalo grass. I hesitated by it for a moment, somewhat disturbed by a few leeches which I could see moving among the grass stems. Then, losing my scruples, I crouched and drank the bitter water. The hollow was sheltered from the wind that had been sweeping endlessly against me as I traveled. I found a dry spot by the water's edge and stretched out to rest a moment. In my exhaustion the minute must have stretched into an hour. Something, some inner alarm, brought me to my senses.

Long shadows were stealing across the pond water and the light was turning red. One of those shadows, I thought dimly, as I tried to move a sleep-stiffened elbow from under my head, seemed to be standing right over me. Drowsily I focused my sight and squinted against the declining sun. In the midst of the shadow I made out a very cold yellow eye and then saw that the thing looming over me was a great blue heron.

He was standing quietly on one foot and looking, like an expert rifleman, down the end of a bill as deadly as an assassin's dagger. I had seen, not long before, a man with his brow split open by a half-grown heron which he had been rash enough to try and capture. The man had been fortunate, for the inexperienced young bird had driven for his eye and missed, gashing his forehead instead.

The bird I faced was perfectly mature and had come softly down on a frog hunt while I slept. Why was he now standing over me? It was certain that momentarily he did not recognize me for a man. Perhaps he was merely curious. Perhaps it was only my little brown eye in the mud he wanted. As this thought penetrated my sleeping brain I rolled, quick as a frog shrieking underfoot, into the water. The great bird, probably as startled as I, rose and beat steadily off into the wind, his long legs folded gracefully behind him.

A little shaken, I stood up and looked after him. There was nothing anywhere for miles and he had come to me like a ghost. How long he had been standing there I do not know. The light was dim now and the cold of the high plains was rising. I shivered and mopped my wet face. The snow on the peak was still visible. I got my bearings and hurried on, determined to make up for lost time. Again the long plain seemed to pass endlessly under my hastening footsteps. For hours I moved under the moon, not too disastrously, though once I fell. The sharp-edged arroyos had appeared again and were a menace in the dark. They were very hard to see, and some were deep.

It was some time after the moon rose that I began to realize that I was being followed. I stopped abruptly and listened.
Something, several things, stopped with me. I heard their feet
put down an instant after mine. Dead silence. "Who's there?" I
said, trying to make the words adjustable and appeasing to any
kind of unwanted companion. There was no answer, though I
had the feel of several shapes just beyond my range of vision.
There was nothing to do. I started on again and the footsteps
began once more, but always they stopped and started with
mine. Finally I began to suspect that the number of my stealthy
followers was growing and that they were closing up the distance between us by degrees.

I had a choice then: I had been realizing it for some time. I
could lose my nerve, run, and invite pursuit, possibly breaking
my leg in a ditch, or, like a sensible human being a little out of
his element perhaps, I could go back and see what threatened
me. On the instant, I stopped and turned.

There was a little clipclop of sound and dead silence once
more, but this time I heard a low uneasy snuffling that could
only come from many noses. I groped in the dark for a stick or a
stone but could find none. I ran three steps back in a threatening
manner and raised a dreadful screech that caused some shuffling
of feet and a little rumble of menacing sound. The screech had
nearly shattered my own nerves. My heart thumped as I tried to
recover my poise.

Cattle.

What was it that gave them this eerie behavior in the dark?

I affected to ignore them. I started on again, whistling, but my mouth was dry. Range cattle, something spelled out in my mind—wild, used to horsemen—what are they like to a man on foot in the dark? They were getting ominously close—that was certain; even if they were just curious, that steady trampling bearing down on my heels was nerve-wracking. Ahead of me at that instant I saw a section of barbed wire against the moon, and behind it a wide boulder-strewn stream bed.

The stream was dry and the starlight shone on the white stones. I swung about and yelled, making a little rush back. Then, without waiting to observe the effects, I turned and openly ran for it. There was a growing thunder behind me. I heard it as I vaulted the fence and landed eight feet down in the sand of the stream bed. Above me I heard a sound like a cavalry troop wheeling off into the night. A braver man might have stood by the fence and waited to see what would happen, but in the night there is this difference that comes over things. I sat on a stone in the stream bed and breathed hard for a long time. Then the chill forced me up again. The arroyo twisted in the direction I was headed. I wandered down it, feeling safer among the stones that reflected light and half-illuminated my path.

A GARDEN BY MOONLIGHT

ELEANOR PERÉNYI

E leanor Perényi (1918–) spent her working life in magazines, first as managing editor of *Mademoiselle*, then as an editor at *Harper's Bazaar*, and as a frequent contributor to *The Atlantic Monthly*, *Harper's*, and *Esquire*. She is the author of an acclaimed biography of Franz Liszt and *More Was Lost* (1946), a memoir of her marriage to an aristocratic Hungarian during the early years of the Second World War. Mostly, however, she is admired as a garden writer. *Green Thoughts: A Writer in the Garden* (1981) is a collection of seventy-two essays on everything horticultural, from "Artichokes" to "A Woman's Place." "Night," reprinted here, is not a survey of such night-blooming plants as cereus and moonflower, but rather an astute comment on the effect of darkness on perception.

. . .

A GARDEN, HOWEVER familiar, is another place on a summer night, and I don't mean those changes wrought by stage designers with "moonlight" and veils—nothing operatic. There are, to begin with, peculiar noises, faint rustlings whose source may be revealed by a flashlight picking up a pair of frozen green eyes. Or the drumming of katydids. Or a sound that occurs in August in a corner of my garden and is answered in the one across the street. In both places, someone seems to be hard at work on a typewriter, clackety-clackety-clack. Answer: clackety-clack. What on earth are they? Not locusts or cicadas, which have a different sound. The most bizarre and least likely explanation yet offered me is that they are raccoons. *Raccoons?* "Well," said the man who told me this, "that's what my cousin who owns the garage out on Route 1 says, and they're all over the back of his place." Why not, when you come to think of it? Perhaps, in lieu of the chimpanzees who one day will write *Hamlet* if the laws of probability are allowed to operate long enough, raccoons are hammering away at *The Theory of the Leisure Class* somewhere in my shrubbery.

Scents are stronger at night. Everybody knows that but not that they are also different. Faint whiffs of sweetness in nicotiana and clethra acquire a dose of pepper after midnight—when, on the other hand, the carnations, at their most powerful at dusk, seem to go to sleep and stop smelling. But the biggest change is that of proportion and texture produced by seeing things in black and white. My first experience of this phenomenon wasn't in the garden, or at night, but in Rome in broad daylight, in the company of a friend who is color-blind. I had always known this about him and never grasped the significance until the day I stupidly said something about the apricot glow of Roman palaces.

"You forget," he said gently, "I don't see that. I don't know what you mean." The words were more than an embarrassment, they were a revelation, for he was the subtlest of observers, who had often pointed out to me details and refinements in paintings and architecture, and even plants, which—blinded in my own way by color—I had missed. Thereafter, I observed things with different and in some ways better-informed eyes, and I haven't forgotten the lesson.

To see things in black and white is to see the basics, and I would now recommend to any designer of gardens that he go out and look at his work by the light of the moon. He may well see that a certain bush is too large for the space it occupies, another too small, that the placement of a flower bed needs adjusting. Above all, he will be more conscious of the importance of form. Strolling among the ruins on the Palatine, my color-blind friend had again and again identified the wild flowers growing there by their shapes, pointing out to me especially the beauty of acanthus, so loved by the Greeks they made it the capital of the Corinthian order, and reminding me that Pliny made beds of acanthus alone, not for the flowers but for the leaves.

The Impressionists saw nature as color swimming in light, but in most of the world's great gardens color has counted for very little. Masses of brilliant shrubs and flowers are a modern idea and not necessarily a good one. Subtract the color from a garden and it can prove to be an ill-planned scramble. One way to find out is to walk around it on a summer night. But not, please, with the aid of floodlight. No matter how skillfully carried out, I abhor the introduction of electricity into a garden. Lighted pools, false dawns among the shrubs are to me both ugly and vulgar. (No. I don't like *son et lumière* either: the Parthenon bathed in lavender is a horrid sight.) A path or driveway may need to be discreetly lighted to keep people from breaking their necks, and hurricane lamps on a terrace where one is dining are more than permissible. I love an old-fashioned Japanese paper lantern stuck with a candle and hung in a tree like a moon. A spotlight trained on a fountain, no. A garden at night should be itself—a place at rest, a haven for creatures, and for me too when I want to lie in the hammock in the dark.

INSECTS THAT
CARRY LANTERNS

A. HYATT VERRILL

Alpheus Hyatt Verrill (1871–1954) led a peripatetic life, beginning as the natural history editor and illustrator for Webster's International Dictionary (1896). In 1902, he invented an autochrome process for natural-colour photography. For ten years, he lived in Dominica, making ethnological and archaeological explorations to the West Indies and Central and South America; in 1907, he rediscovered the hitherto extinct, shrewlike *Solenodon paradoxus* in Santo Domingo. In 1940, he established the Anhiarka Exploratory Gardens and Natural Science Museum in Florida, but he is chiefly remembered as a writer. Author of 105 books, he published science fiction (as Ray Ainsbury), and numerous travel and nature narratives, including a series on creatures of land, sea, and sky. *Strange Insects and Their Stories* (1937) includes this whimsical essay on the then-mysterious firefly.

. . .

THERE IS AN old story of two green Irishmen, newly arrived in America, who were tramping along a country road in search of work one night when they were beset by hordes of mosquitoes. For a time they fought the insects, which were completely new to them, but at last the pests became unbearable, and one of the men suggested that they might escape their tormentors by hiding in a nearby haystack. But still the mosquitoes buzzed and bit. Then one of the men, peering from his hiding place, saw the flashing lights of fireflies. "Sure, Pat," he exclaimed, "'tis niver a bit of use tryin' to hide from thim—they do be afther us with lanterns."

The insects with their "lanterns" which the Irishmen saw were doubtless the common little beetles erroneously called "fireflies." These are soft, rather frail looking creatures with dull colored bodies and heads marked with orange or yellow. There are many species, but all are similar in form and color, although they vary considerably in size and in the amount of light they emit as well as in its color, some giving a clear white light, others a yellow or amber glow, others a greenish light and still others a light of a pinkish tint. Their larvae also possess lights and are commonly known as glowworms, a name which is also applied to the wingless females of some species. Sometimes it is the male beetle who carries the lantern and his mate is lampless or nearly so, in other cases the lady may be the light bearer, while in many species both males and females carry equally bright lights. Although we rarely think of them other than as pretty little creatures whose lights flash and twinkle on summer evenings, yet the fireflies are perhaps the greatest mysteries of Nature, for no one has ever been able to discover how they produce their light.

Great scientists, chemists and countless other investigators have devoted years of study to these tiny insects, striving to solve the riddle, to explain the mystery of the fireflies' light. But the little beetles have baffled them all. Perhaps you wonder why it should be of any importance to discover the secret, but it is difficult to name a discovery which would be of greater importance or of greater benefit to mankind. If the mystery could be solved, and man could duplicate the means by which these insects produce light, just think what it would mean.

It would revolutionize the lighting systems of the world. It would mean cold light of enormous intensity produced with a minimum of power and waste or perhaps without power. In proportion to its size the firefly produces more light than our most powerful dynamos, yet it does not generate a single degree of heat in doing so, and the mechanism or means by which the light is produced is all contained within the tiny space at the tip of the abdomen of the insect. At one time it was thought that the light was some form of phosphorescence. But that theory has been cast aside by many who claim that it is produced by some means akin to electricity, while still others believe it is more similar to the emanations of radio-active chemicals. Viewed in the daytime, the light area of the insect's body appears as a pale-greenish patch of phosphorescent material, and as the light-making portions of all insects which produce light appear the same, we must assume that the waxy, dull whitish-green material must hold the secret. But neither chemical analysis of the material, which is rather spongy or cellular, nor microscopic examinations, have given a clue as to why or how the light should be produced or by what means the insect can turn it on or shut it off at will.

If one single group or class of beetles produced this mysterious light it would be remarkable enough. But the strange power is not confined to one genus or one family or even exclusively to the beetles, but is common to many kinds of insects, although the beetles are the most numerous and most luminous of the insects with lanterns.

Bright and flashing as are the lights of our northern fireflies, they are mere sparks compared to the gleaming lights of many tropical beetles. Most of them are members of the click-beetle or snapping-beetle family and it is a strange fact that while snapping-beetles are very common in the north, and some of their larvae, known as Wire worms, are luminous, yet none of our northern snapping-beetles possess lights when in the adult state. Even stranger is the fact that the tropical light-giving snapping-beetles have two eyes like spots upon the thorax which emit brilliant light, and that some of our northern snapping-beetles have almost identical spots which are not luminous. Why, we wonder, did Nature provide tropical snapping-beetles with a lighting plant and leave the northern members of the group to fly about in darkness with the headlights on their backs mere dummies?

But whatever the reason, Nature made up for our snapping-beetles' lack of lights by giving those of tropical lands lights of incredible power and brilliancy. No one who has never visited the tropics can imagine such fireflies. And even those who have visited tropical lands and have never been in the jungles have no adequate idea of these wonderful insects.

Unlike the lights of our little fireflies, those of the big tropical beetles glow steadily, although the insect may dim his headlights until they are scarcely noticeable or may turn them on with such power and brilliance that ordinary newspaper print may easily be read by the light of a single beetle held above the page. In many places in South America the natives use caged fire beetles for lanterns, and on my expeditions in South and Central America and the West Indies I always keep two or three of these luminous creatures in a small bottle to serve as a flash light at night when I wish to look at my watch. In Costa Rica and other countries as well, the ladies use these big "cucujos" for ornaments in their hair or on their clothing, securing the beetles by means of tiny gold chains or cords attached to the insects' "waists" and with the other end fastened to a pin. As the beetles crawl about, flashing their radiant lights in the dark hair of the women or on the lace of their garments, they are very beautiful and appear like living jewels, for the lights are of various colors—white, green, yellow or red—according to the species of the insects.

Although when crawling about or when at rest, the brilliant light of these beetles shines from the eye-like spots upon the thorax, the entire body is luminous and it is the motion of the insects' wings in flight—alternately hiding and exposing the glowing abdomen beneath the wings, which gives the effect of flashing lights.

No one who has watched thousands of these insects flitting about the edge of a tropical forest or in the vegetation bordering a jungle stream will ever forget the sight. There is nothing like it on all the earth, no sight to equal it, a sight as indescribable as it is wonderful.

It is not surprising that when the Spaniards approached the southern coast of Cuba and saw myriads of these great fire beetles twinkling and flashing on the shores they mistook the insects for Indians with firebrands and named it Cienfuegos, or the place of a hundred fires, although Milfuegos or a thousand fires would have been more appropriate.

On another occasion the fireflies or rather firebeetles served the Spaniards a mighty good turn. This was when Sir Thomas Cavendish was stealthily approaching a Spanish settlement trusting to a surprise attack to win a victory. But seeing the big fireflies moving about, he and his men mistook them for torches in the hands of the Dons and thinking his approach had been discovered and the Spaniards were prepared to resist, he abandoned the attack and returning to his ships sailed away.

Remarkable as are these great tropical insects with their brilliant lights, the most wonderful of all and the most surprising as well, is the larva of one of these big beetles. Several inches in length, this caterpillar-like creature carries a whole row of brilliant greenish-white lights on either side of its body, while a reddish light gleams faintly from the tip of its tail and twin golden-yellow lights flash from its head.

As the insect crawls among the weeds or grass, twisting and turning on its erratic course, it is the exact counterpart of a Lilliputian railway train, and throughout the Guianas, in Venezuela and Brazil, in fact wherever it is found, it is always known as the Railway worm, whether the name is in Spanish, Portuguese, Dutch, French or English. Only the native Indians, who of course never even heard of a railway until long after the white men arrived, have a different name for this strange insect. They call it the Metacusi worm. As Metacusi is the name of an Indian dance in which the dancers carry torches and form a procession that twists and turns in imitation of a huge serpent, the Indians' name for the strangest of insect light carriers is just as appropriate as that bestowed upon it by the white men.

BATS

CHARLES BOWDEN

Charles Bowden (1945–) began writing as a crime reporter for the Tucson *Citizen*. To escape the violence of his day job, he would hike alone in the desert, which he chronicled in *Blue Desert* (1986), excerpted here. In *Inferno, Down by the River, Frog Mountain Blues,* and more than a dozen other books, Bowden continued to explore the darker side of life, both human and natural—a distinction he refuses to make. Instrumental in creating the Sonoran Desert National Monument, he writes, "We need these places not to remember our better selves or our natural self or our spiritual self. We need these places to taste what we fear and devour what we are. We need these places to be animals, because unless we are animals we are nothing at all."

. . .

THE AIR SCREAMS, rustling movements feather against the skin, squeaks and screeches bounce off the stone walls, and a sweet acrid stench rolls across the room. My mouth chews the darkness like a thick paste.

We stand in feces, hills of feces, and the grey powder slops over our running shoes and buries our ankles. Behind us the light glows through the cave entrance, a slit sixty-five feet high and twenty-four feet wide. Above us the screams continue, the rustling frolic of life. The rock walls feel like cloth to the touch; a wilderness of fungus thrives in the warm room.

We climb. The hills of feces roll like trackless dunes. Our feet sink deeply into the grey powder as we move up toward the ceiling. Here and there a feather: a primary off a turkey vulture; a secondary off a black hawk. There is no explanation for their presence. The odor seems to ebb as our senses adjust to the stench. The dunes toss like waves and in between the dark mounds writhe masses of beetle larvae. Here we find the bones—skulls, femurs, rib cages, and the like.

This is the forbidden place, the dark zone claimed by nightmares. The air can be rich with rabies and people and animals have died from visiting such places. Up high, up near the ceiling, the rustling grows louder and louder. They are disturbed as we march into their world. The eye sees blackness but the skin feels the rustling, the swoosh of something near our brows, our throats, our mouths. We are enveloped in a swirling mass of energy and we keep walking toward the center of this biological bomb.

Something is crawling up our bare legs, across our bellies, down our arms, past our necks and onward into the curious contours of our faces. Mites move up from the dunes of feces and explore us like a new country. When we pause and look up, our eyes peer into a mist, a steady drizzle of urine and feces cascading from the ceiling.

I have no desire to leave. The feces and urine continue to shower down, the mites tickle the surface of my body, the atmosphere tastes like a bad meal and always the air drifting like a thick fog promises the whisper of rabies.

We have come to the charnel house, a bastion of a world in the twilight of life. The crackling energy swirling in the air around us is dying. And we and our kind are the killers.

This is the bat cave and 25,000 *Tadarida brasiliensis mexicana* wrap us with their anxiety. Night is falling outside the cave. Soon our world will become theirs.

Then they will exit and plunder the canyons, the mesas, the hillsides, the towns, the fields. They will bring back deadly reports of our world, details buried deep in their bones and body chemistry.

The sound tightens now, a shrill spike of screeches and squeaks. The mites scramble across the skin. The larvae writhe like shiny stones at our feet.

We stand inside a brief island of life, a hiding place of our blood kin.

WE HAVE known each other a good long while. We would pluck the eye of a live bat, stick it in a wax figure of a dog, put the effigy at a crossroads and hope a lover would come to our bed. We would make an ointment of frankincense, the blood of a lizard, the blood of a bat and treat trachoma. We would carve the image of a bat on the tip of a rhinoceros horn to ward off demons. We would cut the head off a live bat and place it on someone's left arm to cause insomnia. We would crucify live bats, heads downward, always downward and place the result over our doors to fight evil, to protect our sleep, to insure our wakefulness.

We have hated bats. We still hate bats. They own the night and mock our helplessness. Their faces to our eyes look cruel, fierce, ugly.

For thousands of years, they rode through our dreams, they drank our blood, they stood as symbols of a world we were reluctant to enter but a place we lusted for—the black nights, the witches' sabbaths, the magic chants, the scream under a full moon . . .

Like us, they are mammals. Their blood is warm and they nurse their young. One out of every five species of mammals is a bat. Forty-five million years before the first beast that looked like a human being walked this earth, bats took to the sky. The early bat jumped from tree to tree after insects and over time the arm became the wing and the air became a new floor for life.

Eight hundred fifty species now swirl across the planet's skin and twenty-four can be found in Arizona. *Tadarida brasiliensis mexicana,* the Mexican free-tail, roams from Texas westward and winters deep in Mexico. This small bat rides on a wingspan of about a foot. The hair runs from dark brown to dark gray. They favor caves—thirteen in Texas, five in Oklahoma and one each in New Mexico, Arizona and Nevada.

These hunters search the desert and sometimes feed as high as 9,200 feet. They can live in colonies of millions, huge masses of bats squeaking, chattering, and crawling across each other. When big colonies once exited from their caves, the sound, according to early observers, thundered like the roar of white water and the dark cloud could be seen for miles. They fly into the night at about thirty-five miles per hour, then accelerate to around sixty. At dawn, they make power dives back into the cave, sometimes brushing eighty miles per hour.

They feed on small moths, ripping the abdomens from them in flight, and may travel forty miles in any direction seeking prey. The young, one per female per year, immediately crawl up the mother hunting the breast. At first, the mother returns several times during the night to nurse and then less frequently. No one is certain if the females find their own young in the huge colonies or nurse the first young bat they encounter. They can live perhaps fifteen years—no one is sure.

Bats remain a mystery in many ways. Science has come to them late in the day. They have been banded and migrations of 1,000 miles recorded. They have been kidnapped and released to test their homing instincts and a return of 328 miles has been observed.

And they have been dying. Oklahoma had 7 million Mexican free-tails and is now down to fewer than 1 million. Carlsbad Caverns had around 9 million and is down to 250,000. And the cave on the creek in the canyon near Clifton and Morenci had its 25 million or perhaps even 50 million and is down to 25,000 or fewer . . .

Outside green blazes off the trees and the stream slides like a brown skin over the rocks. Light ebbs from the canyon. We climb down from the dunes of guano, slip off the rock shelves to the cave opening. The night begins to come down.

Ronnie holds a feather and the delicate finger bone of a bat. And then it begins.

"Oh, my God," she says. "Oh, look at them all. This is great!"

Urine and feces rain down on us. We look up and cannot look away. Bats storm across the top of the vault, a torrent of wings and squeaks. They streak to the canyon center and swirl and then funnel off. This is the major flight. The free-tails give a faint echo of the thunder of twenty years ago when perhaps 100 million tiny mammals squealed from the room in the rock wall and took to the night sky, an army of heart, lungs, and fangs ranging out twenty, thirty, forty miles, beasts ripping the soft abdomens from moths, feasting in the dark hours.

A crescent moon hangs and the bats become fine lines etching the glowing face. In four minutes, it is over. A flight that once took hours is now 240 seconds. The cave falls silent.

They are gone.

NIGHT-LIFE AT PEAK HILL

LOUISE DE KIRILINE LAWRENCE

Louise de Kiriline Lawrence (1894–1992) was born in Sweden to an aristocratic family. Provoked by the First World War, she became a nurse
and married a White Russian, who was imprisoned in Siberia following the
Revolution. Upon his death, she emigrated to Canada, where she worked
as a Red Cross nurse in northern Ontario, travelling by dogsled to the sick.
Among her patients were the Dionne quintuplets, whom she nursed for a
year. Appalled by the publicity surrounding them, she retreated to a log
cabin on the Mattawa River, where she studied birds and wildlife. A regular
contributor to *Audubon Magazine*, she wrote more than five hundred articles and five books, including *The Lovely and the Wild*, which won the John
Burroughs Medal, making her the first woman to be so honoured.

. . .

PEAK HILL TOWERS above Pimisi Bay and is the highest hill
in the vicinity. Below, the lake looks like blue glass cut out to fit
the irregular shoreline. On dewy mornings light mists mark the

course of the Mattawa River amongst the blueing hills beyond the lake. On the other side of the Trans-Canada Highway the house nestles under the pines.

It was down there that the whippoorwills had chosen the rock outside our bedroom window as their courtship bower. Every night since the male's first ringing call sounded his return in early May, he came there to proclaim his territorial aspirations. He sat there crouched, his head low, rocking his body gently from side to side, calling loudly over and over again, *chuck-whip-poor-will, chuck-whip-poor-will, chuck-whip-poor-will*!

But one day the male's calling abruptly changed. At the end of a prolonged sentence the even tempo of his singing was suddenly accelerated to breathless speed.

I crept up to the window. The male was no longer alone. The dim shape of another whippoorwill wheeled down upon the rock and crouched close beside him. It was the female. She lacked the flashing white of the male's breastband and tail feathers. And from then on wherever they were I could tell when the male was no longer alone.

He pressed himself up to her. *Coorah, coorah,* he uttered. He swooped up into the air, displaying, and down on her other side. But she only pressed her breast against the ground. He bowed from side to side and his *coorah* dissolved into cooings, soft, fast, softer, faster.

But the stirrings of her blood did not yet match his. She flew and the male followed in great excitement. On the way he became distracted by a large June bug that buzzed around a tree-top. He dashed in pursuit, hovered an instant like a huge hummingbird on wings beating at invisible speed, caught the insect in his enormous whiskered mouth and disappeared from sight.

A week later I came upon the female sitting alone on the rock. Over the lake a full moon was rising like a giant golden coin. I stood perfectly still, and a moment later the male alighted on another rock at some distance from the female. He cooed softly, flashed the white of his tail feathers. She did not move where she sat not five feet in front of me. Silently the male flew up behind her. She crouched deeper, spread her wings. Lightly, like a butterfly, he descended upon her. Wings rippled, trembled. Then both birds disappeared into the shadows of the trees.

It was apparently the eggs of this pair that I stumbled upon at Peak Hill. An opportunity so rarely granted, I decided to learn more of this bird which sings and mates and lives in the night. For the purpose, I arranged a blind some 10 feet away from the bird, a green-mottled blanket with slits torn in convenient places. Behind it I tucked a folding chair into a young fir tree and covered up my backview with fresh spruce boughs.

That evening, with a flashlight, a watch, and a potent insecticide, I climbed up Peak Hill and slunk as noiselessly as I could into my shelter. The sun, round and flame-red, was just sinking below the horizon. In the twilight, the trees lost their green color and stood like darkened silhouettes against the orange-green sky.

The whippoorwill was sitting motionless on her eggs, like a small mound of dead leaves. She sat just in front of the fallen spruce trunk and a few sprigs of its dead top branches reached out over her. From above, her brown-speckled feather-dress made her invisible and from my blind I had to convince myself she actually was where I knew her to be. She slept with her head tucked under one wing.

All around us the song of the birds had gone into the mighty finale of the day. A hermit thrush was singing from a red pine afire in the last beam of the sun. From time to time ovenbirds rose in exuberant flight songs, brilliantly hued magnolia, myrtle and Nashville warblers flitted from tree to tree, singing, and a bejewelled Canada warbler successfully held his own in the stiff competition. Behind me three Wilson's thrushes challenged the hermit's masterpieces with their golden strains descending the scale.

In my darkened shelter a few black flies hummed against the ceiling, trying to escape the air poisoned by the sprayer. A little deer mouse startled me with the rustle of its feet as it scampered over a rotten log and nervously slipped down a friendly hole further away.

It grew darker. A couple of fireflies flashed their tail-lights across the shadows like tiny comets. The whippoorwill sat on her eggs, deathly still.

Then it happened. From out of the woods behind me an apparition flashed into view. It was the male. He looked like a huge moth, much larger than he really was. His spread tail feathers shone startlingly white. Without a sound he wheeled down towards the female. He alighted in front of her. He pressed his breast to the earth, he edged up to her until bill met bill and he became a perfect looking-glass image of her. He uttered a caressing *coorah, coorah*—long-drawn, deliciously tender. He seemed to feed her, but the darkness prevented me from seeing the details of his action. He remained thus in front of her for fully three minutes.

By their eyes, shining red like miniature Chinese lanterns, I could follow the movements of the birds with my flashlight. The illumination did not seem to disturb them. Noiselessly the female flew off her eggs, and it was the first time I saw her leave them of her own volition. The male took her place, turning around tail south. Immovable, he remained on the eggs for a long time.

But presently the male's eyes began to move. He left the eggs which, uncovered, shone white on their pine-needle bed. A second later I heard them calling from Green Woods down below. He tore the silence to shreds. From south, east and west, neighbouring whippoorwills answered him.

The next time I visited Peak Hill it was an hour before dawn. I stumbled through the thick underbrush and climbed the hill guided by my flashlight.

Suddenly, in the pitch darkness, an ovenbird flung himself above the tree-tops in the most magnificent flight song I have ever heard and fell to earth again I knew not where. A couple of whippoorwills called in the distance.

In the beam of the flashlight the humped outline of the whippoorwill showed faintly, her eyes shining red. The woods were sopping wet after a thunderstorm and the mosquitoes were murderous. I sat on my rickety chair writing my notes by feel.

At this early hour the ovenbirds seemed to be moved by some special exultation, for from the woods below, bird after bird rose in thrilling flight song.

A little breeze rustled through the leaves, and died just as a faint light began to show on the horizon. With rare inspiration a hermit thrush began to sing. Then a song sparrow suddenly burst into song. The Wilson's thrushes awakened and a white-throated sparrow surprised the world with the clearest whistle. A little while later a robin gave a *sotto voce* rendering of its theme to begin the day's activity, and from all corners of the land, whippoorwills called vigorously as if they, too, belonged to the daylight parade.

I did not see her go, but as I flashed on my light the whippoorwill was gone. Alone, I sat there and listened to the rising volume of bird song as dawn seeped in through the trees. Every bird was soon awake and singing. There was no movement, only song.

SKUNK DREAMS

LOUISE ERDRICH

ouise Erdrich (1954–) was raised in North Dakota, the daughter of Ger-
man and Anishinaabe teachers and granddaughter to the tribal chair-
man of the Turtle Mountain Band of Chippewa Indians. Associated with
the landscape of the Great Plains as surely as Faulkner is with the South,
Erdrich's novels explore the lives of a cluster of fictional families living
in and around the Turtle Mountain/Pembina reservation. *The Blue Jay's
Dance* (1995), from which this passage is taken, is a rare work of nonfiction:
a memoir of her first year with a child. A writer of keen poetic sensibility
and a sharp observer of both nature and human nature, Erdrich excels at the
telling moment, forged here into a forthright, impassioned recollection of
motherhood. As she says, "Any sublime effort has its dark moments."

. . .

WHEN I WAS fourteen, I slept alone on a North Dakota football field under cold stars on an early September night. Fall pro-
gresses swiftly in the Red River Valley, and I happened to hit a

night when frost formed in the grass. A skunk trailed a plume of steam across the forty-yard line near moonrise. I tucked the top of my sleeping bag over my head and was just dozing off when the skunk walked onto me with simple authority.

Its ripe odor must have dissipated in the heavy summer grass and ditch weeds, because it didn't smell all that bad, or perhaps it was just that I took shallow breaths in numb surprise. I felt him, her, whatever, pause on the side of my hip and turn around twice before evidently deciding I was a good place to sleep. At the back of my knees, on the quilting of my sleeping bag, it trod out a spot for itself and then, with a serene little groan, curled up and lay perfectly still. That made two of us. I was wildly awake, trying to forget the sharpness and number of skunk teeth, trying not to think of the high percentage of skunks with rabies, or the reason that on camping trips my father always kept a hatchet underneath his pillow.

Inside the bag, I felt as if I might smother. Carefully, making only the slightest of rustles, I drew the bag away from my face and took a deep breath of the night air, enriched with skunk, but clear and watery and cold. It wasn't so bad, and the skunk didn't stir at all, so I watched the moon—caught that night in an envelope of silk, a mist—pass over my sleeping field of teenage guts and glory. The grass harbored a sere dust both old and fresh. I smelled the heat of spent growth beneath the rank tone of my bag-mate—the stiff fragrance of damp earth and the thick pungency of newly manured fields a mile or two away—along with my sleeping bag's smell, slightly mildewed, forever smoky.

The skunk settled even closer and began to breathe rapidly; its feet jerked a little like a dog's. I sank against the earth, and fell asleep too.

Of what easily tipped cans, what molten sludge, what dogs in yards on chains, what leftover macaroni casseroles, what cellar holes, crawl spaces, burrows taken from meek woodchucks, of what miracles of garbage did my skunk dream? Or did it, since we can't be sure, dream the plot of *Moby-Dick,* how to properly age Parmesan, or how to restore the brick-walled tumble-down creamery that was its home? We don't know about the dreams of any other biota, and even much about our own. If dreams are an actual dimension, as some assert, then the usual rules of life by which we abide do not apply. In that place, skunks may certainly dream themselves into the vests of stockbrokers. Perhaps that night the skunk and I dreamed each other's thoughts or are still dreaming them. To paraphrase the problem of the Taoist philosopher Chuang Tzu, I may be a woman who has dreamed herself a skunk, or a skunk still dreaming that she is a woman.

In a book called *Death and Consciousness,* David H. Lund—who wants very much to believe in life after death—describes human dream life as a possible model for a disembodied existence.

"Many of one's dreams," he says, "are such that they involve the activities of an apparently embodied person whom one takes to be oneself as long as one dreams . . . Whatever is the source of the imagery . . . apparently has the capacity to bring about images of a human body and to impart the feeling that the body is mine. It is, of course, just an image body, but it serves as a perfectly good body for the dream experience. I regard it as mine, I act on the dream environment by means of it, and it constitutes the center of the perceptual world of my dream."

OVER THE years I have acquired and reshuffled my beliefs and doubts about whether we live on after death—in any shape or form, that is, besides the molecular level at which I am to be absorbed by the taproots of cemetery elms or pines and the tangled mats of fearfully poisoned, too green lawn grass. I want something of the self on whom I have worked so hard to survive the loss of the body (which, incidentally, the self has done a fairly decent job of looking after, excepting spells of too much cabernet and a few idiotic years of rolling my own cigarettes out of Virginia Blond tobacco). I am put out with the marvelous discoveries of the intricate biochemical configuration of our brains, though I realize that the processes themselves are quite miraculous. I understand that I should be self-proud, content to geewhiz at the fact that I am the world's only mechanism that can admire itself. I should be grateful that life is here today, though gone tomorrow, but I can't help it. I want more.

SKUNKS DON'T mind each other's vile perfume. Obviously, they find each other more than tolerable. And even I, who have been in the presence of a direct skunk hit, wouldn't classify their weapon as mere smell. It is more on the order of a reality-enhancing experience. It's not so pleasant as standing in a grove of old-growth cedars, or on a lyrical moonshed plain, or watching trout rise to the shadow of your hand on the placid surface of an Alpine lake. When the skunk lets go, you're surrounded by skunk presence: inhabited, owned, involved with something you can only describe as powerfully *there*.

I woke at dawn, stunned into that sprayed state of being. The dog that had approached me was rolling in the grass, half addled, sprayed too. My skunk was gone. I abandoned my sleeping bag and started home. Up Eighth Street, past the tiny blue and pink houses, past my grade school, past all the addresses where I baby-sat, I walked in my own strange wind. The streets were wide and empty; I met no one—not a dog, not a squirrel, not even an early robin. Perhaps they had all scattered before me, blocks away. I had gone out to sleep on the football field because I was afflicted with a sadness I had to dramatize. Mood swings had begun, hormones, feverish and raw. They were nothing to me now. My emotions had seemed vast, dark, and sickeningly private. But they were minor, mere wisps, compared to skunk.

THE LIGHT THAT FAILED

———

Grey Owl, or Wa-Sha-Quon-Asin, was the alter ego of Archie Belaney (1888–1938), a British-born immigrant to Canada obsessed with wilderness and native culture. Through his Iroquois wife, he became aware of the disappearing forest ecosystem and, in 1931, was hired as the first naturalist for the Dominion Parks system. He began to write, publishing seven books under his native pseudonym, including the classic *Tales of an Empty Cabin* (1936), excerpted here. He toured North America and Europe extensively, dressed in full Indian regalia; his true identity was discovered only at his death, causing an uproar that obliterated, for a time, his contribution to conservation. It was his acute powers of observation, evident in this piece, that earned him the name of that shy creature of the night.

. . .

I HAVE NEVER been lost. The fact that I am here at Beaver Lodge proves it; when a man is lost there is an end to it. Never have I used a compass or any other mechanical or scientific device in travelling known or unknown territory, and never will; yet I have never been lost—but I have been "turned around," lost my bearings for a time, had sometimes to do some pretty fast calculating. A man who says he never was "turned around," as we call this state of affairs in our manner of speech, is either a prevaricator or else he never travelled very much in the woods.

The word "lost" is open to a good many different interpretations, and quite the best of these that I have heard, was the one given by an old bushwhacker, who for some inexplicable reason, became so twisted in his calculations that it took ten men over a week to find him; he would not plead guilty to having been lost; no sir; he wasn't lost, not he; but he had been "right bewildered"—for eight days!

And now I'll tell one.

As my name indicates, I have a decided liking, and some aptitude, for travelling at night. Not that my eyes are particularly adapted for seeing in the dark, or are especially piercing or capable of projecting any gleaming rays of light into the gloom of a midnight forest. Not that at all. Simply this, that not ten per cent of nights are really dark; and to one who is accustomed to night work, the darkness seems a few shades lighter than to the ordinary person. A man may cover a lot of territory, even strange territory, in the dark if he has a good, comprehensive knowledge of wilderness travel in general, a reliable sense of direction, a sensitive pair of ears, and a kind of nervous alertness that apprises him of what is going on around him; moreover he must be able to "feel" the lay of the land, and above all, he must feel perfectly at home, and not allow the fact that he is alone in the dark, in a wild country, to get under his skin.

Aside from all the above, the matter is quite simple. There's nothing to it. I have travelled through heavy forests in what would pass for complete darkness (but wasn't really), and in only a very few instances have I been compelled to use birch-bark torches to accomplish this. I have paddled over long routes, entire nights at a time, including the crossing of numerous por-tages with canoe and load, at a pace little less than that attained in daylight hours, and have both run down and poled up rapids at night by the sound of them, assisted somewhat by the blurred gleam of the starlight on wet rocks and on the white-crested breakers.

All very clever, if not actually uncanny, thinks you; and in such subdued light, or absence of it, these feats may seem to be unusual. However, they are commonly performed without undue self-commendation, by men of my calling. Such exploits excite small comment, and are expected. But there is such a thing as having too much light, when it will create a confusion far greater than could have been occasioned by any amount of darkness; and to this odd predicament I once fell a facile and very humiliated victim.

On a winter night, far in the wilderness of Northern Quebec, my trapping partner, who had never been a soldier, demanded some stories of the war. Like most of those who saw active ser-vice on any front, my reminiscences ran more to thoughts of

vermin, mud and short rations than to fighting. So vivid were
my portrayals of the deprivations endured, that I talked the two
of us into a practically starving condition. Having that morning
killed a deer only a short distance from the cabin, I decided to
go out at once and get some of the meat, while my partner said
he would in the meantime make a bannock. It was very dark,
and as I would have to skin the deer I took along a lantern.

Never before had I travelled in the woods by means of artificial light, save on a trail, there being none in this case as a
heavy snowstorm had obliterated whatever tracks I had made
on my way home from the deer; and there befell me just what I
had always heard would happen to any man who attempted to
find his way in the bush with a light—I couldn't find my objective. The deer was probably three hundred yards away, and I
had started in the right direction. But lanterns have a fashion of
throwing their glare in circles, which had the effect of intensify-
ing the encircling darkness, so that everything beyond a radius
of a dozen feet was black as the bottomless pit, and nothing outside of it was visible.

After going on for some time without finding the deer, I now
discovered something else—a snowshoe track, going my way.
In the deep, loose snow, the outline of the shoe was blurred and
more or less shapeless, and I could not identify it. Now there
was supposed to be no one but ourselves in the country; my own
previous tracks were snowed under, so this called for investiga-
tion, which I decided to make later. I turned off short towards
the deer, and went a considerable distance without encountering

it; but I *did* find another set of snowshoe prints, this time crossing mine. I didn't know what to think of this, but went on looking for my kill, feeling, rather ashamedly, that I had shown some
very poor scout-craft in so over-shooting my mark. I swung off
a little, only to run slap into, not one snowshoe trail, but two
of them. Both of these veered off to my right, and crossing one
another ran into a third, and within a short distance, yet a fourth
set of impressions. And all at once I seemed to be surrounded by
tracks, and try as I might, I could in no way get clear of this
maze of snowshoe trails by which I seemed to be beleaguered.
All were going the same way, to the right—who the devil were
these trespassers careering around in this senseless, circuituous
steeplechase! I went after them at a round trot, but they crossed
their own trails, again to the right, and eluded me. I stopped and
listened; but everything was silent as the grave, enveloped in
the padded hush that pervades the winter wilderness, especially
at night. The whole thing began to be a trifle spooky.

I cantered on, leaping and bounding along in great style; this
went on for some time, and then I found that the other fellows
(there were now four of them) must have heard me, as they were
also leaping and bounding along, as their marks plainly showed,
in what now amounted to a whole drove of people. I was never
so exasperated in my life, and continued the pursuit on my big
snowshoes, the light of the lantern throwing my huge shadow,
huge and distorted, against the background of the snow-bound
trees, like a gigantic hob-goblin who grotesquely pranced
beside me and followed with fantastical fidelity my every action.

I seemed, within the orbit of my circle of lantern light, to be confined in a deep, illuminated pit, that walled me round and moved with me as I went, and the adventure was not without an eerie aspect of unreality. Entertained by the fanciful notion that this might after all be only a dream, (and having had, for the last while back, certain well founded suspicions) I became a little inattentive, and fell headlong over a large snow mound. The lantern was saved from going out by some gymnastics that would have done credit to a professional acrobat, and by the light of it I saw, sticking out of the mound of snow, the hoof of some animal.

I had at last arrived at my deer; and looking around I observed that all the men I had been chasing had arrived there also. There were just two—my shadow and myself.

In the woods at night, an artificial light will fool you every time; every way you face is straight ahead, and no bearings can be taken, especially from above, where the outline of the tree-tops is nearly always discernible, and of great help; and so, enclosed above, below, and on all sides, in a globe of light as it were, one is apt to travel round and round in a very circumscribed area. This I had done, my own tracks increasing in number as I overtook myself, so to speak, the circles getting smaller and smaller, until I had about wound myself down to a point. Taking some meat, I then unwound myself back again to the cabin, feeling rather subdued, to find my partner asleep and the bannock cold. I awoke him, being by now determined to eat deer-meat on this night of our Lord if it killed the two of us.

And as we ate, my partner was from time to time obliged to turn his back and emit gurgling and suppressed choking noises that were quite unnecessary, and annoyed me considerably.

And I leave it to you to decide whether it was the light that failed me, or I that failed the light.

IN THE DARK

PICO IYER

Pico Iyer (1957–) was born in Britain of Indian parents who immigrated to California while Iyer was still in school. Thus began the travels that led him to call himself a "multinational soul on a multinational globe." In 1995, *Utne Reader* magazine named him one of one hundred visionaries who "could change your life." As well as two novels, Iyer has written seven works of nonfiction that turn on close observation of contained societies. In *Sun After Dark: Flights into the Foreign* (2004), from which this piece is taken, Iyer infuses exotic adventure with provocative, fundamental questions. For the traveller, he writes, "day is stretched and stretched, in this foreign world of displacement, till it snaps." The night is peeled back, revealing "something more odorous and ancient, less domesticated."

. . .

IT WAS DARK when I set foot on the island, and it felt as if the darkness was chattering. I could see oil lamps flickering at the edges of the forest. I could hear the gamelan coming from somewhere inside the trees, clangorous, jangled, and hypnotic. I could see people by the side of the road as I drove in from the airport, but I couldn't tell how many there were, or what they were doing in the dark. When I woke up, jet-lagged, in the dead of night, and walked down to the beach, figures came out of the shadows to offer me "jig-jig" or some other amenity of Paradise. There was a holy cave on the island, I had read, inhabited only by bats; there was a temple in the sea guarded by a snake.

The bush is burning only for those who are completely foreign to it, I had often thought; in the works of V.S. Naipaul, say, the jungle is seldom a force of magic, and if it is, it speaks for a magic that is only pushing back and down the clear daylight world of reason. Those born to nature seldom have to go back to it. Yet in Bali all these ideas are upended. Bali is a magical world for those who can see its invisible forces and read all the unseen currents in the air (that woman is a *leyak* witch, and that shade of green portends death). Yet for everyone else, it is simple enchantment. We stand at the gates of Eden, looking in, and choose to forget that one central inhabitant of the Garden is a snake.

I walked through the unfallen light my first day in Bali, to the beach, to watch, as foreigners do, the sun sink into the sea. Snake-armed masseuses were putting their things away for the day and boys were kicking a soccer ball into the coloring waves. As the outlines of the place began to fade, and the dark to take over, a woman came up to me and asked if I'd like to take a walk with her.

I couldn't really see her in the dark, and the name she gave me—Wayan—is the same name given to the oldest son or daughter of every family on the island. It was pitch-black as we walked along the sand, and pitch-black when we turned into what I thought was the little lane that led back to my guest house. At night in Bali, the dogs come out, and they are nothing like the serene creatures who sit outside the temples of Tibet, seeming to guard the monks. The dogs in Bali howl and curse and bite. As we walked through the forest on the path back to where I slept, I could feel the dogs very close to us, and everywhere.

We know Bali, those of us who read about it, as a magic island where there are thirty thousand temples in a space not much bigger than a major city; we have heard that it is a forest of the kind you see in *A Midsummer Night's Dream,* where people fall in love with the first Other that they meet. A childhood friend of mine had had her first real experience of real transport with a stranger in a thatched hut on Kuta Beach; all around, you can see what look like asses—or rude mechanicals—waiting to be picked up by Titania.

But the stranger at my side did not seem interested only in romance as she led me up into the heart of her island's cosmology of light and dark. We walked along the buzzing lanes of Kuta after dark, dogs growling on every side. We walked along a beach on the other side of the island, where couples are supposed to walk on full-moon nights. We took a ride up into the interior, where whole villages are given over to ritual dance: small girls were fluttering their bare arms in the temple courtyards, and boys were chattering in a trance. Foreigners often awaken in the night in Bali to see ghosts standing by their beds; when a brother needs to communicate with a brother, a Balinese dancer once told me, with no drama in his voice, he finds telepathy easier than the telephone.

I walked through all these spaces with the girl from the beach, and through the skepticism I brought to them, and felt at times we were walking through parallel worlds: she could read everything around us, and I could read nothing. This was the way people were buried on the island, she said; this was why black magicians lived in that forest of monkeys. Part of the excitement of being a foreigner in a place like Bali is that you can't reduce the signs around you to an everyday language.

That is also what is unsettling about being a foreigner in a place like Bali, and after some days I slipped away from the girl, and went to the airport, to fly away. When I got there, she was standing at the gate, come, she said, to say goodbye. We would not meet again, she went on, because she had dreamed the previous night that she would put on a white dress and go across what is the Balinese equivalent of the Styx.

THIS IS the kind of mystery that makes an almost ideal souvenir: something strange and a little spooky that you can take back to your regular life in (as it was for me then) Rockefeller Center. When I chanced to return to Bali, eighteen months later, I took pains not to tell Wayan I was coming, and to make my way discreetly back to the little lane where I'd stayed before. But when

I came out of my guest house the first night back, at dusk, there she was, waiting, at the threshold, as if we had made a prior arrangement.

We went out again into the dark, the unlit fields behind the night market, the lanes that seemed, after dark, to be inhabited only by dogs. It was better to meet in broad daylight, I told her, and made a date to get together on the public beach at noon. She was wearing a sky-blue dress when I met her there, not scarlet as before, and her manner was withdrawn. I wasn't here for very long, I said, I didn't know where we were going: all the visitor's easy evasions. She looked at me, and then it was goodbye.

When I went back to my little room, I was unable to move. For days on end, I couldn't stir. I wasn't feverish, and yet something in me was waterlogged, leaden. I couldn't step out of my hut to eat or drink or take a walk; I couldn't sleep. For three days I lay on my bed and listened to the dogs amidst the trees, the gamelan. An Australian was pressing his claim on a local girl in the next room and she, laughing, was dancing away. I saw lizards on the walls of my room, and I awoke one morning to find that the lizard was nothing but a light switch. I went up into the hills, summoning all my strength for the one-hour trip, but something in me was evacuated: a guardian spirit vanished in the night.

It was time to leave the enchanted island, I decided. But before I did, I wanted something to remind me that I had been here, and that all of this had really happened: proof, of a kind. The streets of Bali teem with masks, which hang from the fronts of stores, staring-eyed, with tongues protruding, as talismans of the island's nighttime ceremonies. Knowing that they were too potent to take back home, I looked for something more innocuous, and found an owl.

I took the owl back with me to my small studio apartment in Manhattan and put it up on my wall. Almost instantly the New York night was so full of chatterings and hauntings that I had to get up and rip the thing down, and put it away in a closet where I'd never have to lay eyes on it again. You go into the dark to get away from what you know, and if you go far enough, you realize, suddenly, that you'll never really make it back into the light.

NIGHT LIFE

TIM O'BRIEN

Tim O'Brien (1946–) was born in western Minnesota, a landscape that
figures prominently in many of his books. Although a war protester,
he fought in Vietnam, an experience he recounts in his memoir, *If I Die
in a Combat Zone; Box Me Up and Ship Me Home* (1973), one of the first
books about that war written by a combatant. An infantryman, he served
in the region around My Lai shortly after the massacre, which is central
to his novel *In the Lake of the Woods* (1994). He has written six other novels, often traversing the no-man's-land between fact and fiction. *The Things
They Carried* (1990), excerpted here, returns to Vietnam, where the long,
dark night of the soul is both a physical and a metaphorical place.

. . .

A FEW WORDS about Rat Kiley. I wasn't there when he got
hurt, but Mitchell Sanders later told me the essential facts.
Apparently he lost his cool.

The platoon had been working an AO out in the foothills west
of Quang Ngai City, and for some time they'd been receiving

intelligence about an NVA buildup in the area. The usual crazy rumors: massed artillery and Russian tanks and whole divisions of fresh troops. No one took it seriously, including Lieutenant Cross, but as a precaution the platoon moved only at night, staying off the main trails and observing strict field SOPs. For almost two weeks, Sanders said, they lived the night life. That was the phrase everyone used: the night life. A language trick. It made things seem tolerable. How's the Nam treating you? one guy would ask, and some other guy would say, Hey, one big party, just living the night life.

It was a tense time for everybody, Sanders said, but for Rat Kiley it ended up in Japan. The strain was too much for him. He couldn't make the adjustment.

During those two weeks the basic routine was simple. They'd sleep away the daylight hours, or try to sleep, then at dusk they'd put on their gear and move out single file into the dark. Always a heavy cloud cover. No moon and no stars. It was the purest black you could imagine, Sanders said, the kind of clock-stopping black that God must've had in mind when he sat down to invent blackness. It made your eyeballs ache. You'd shake your head and blink, except you couldn't even tell you were blinking, the blackness didn't change. So pretty soon you'd get jumpy. Your nerves would go. You'd start to worry about getting cut off from the rest of the unit—alone, you'd think—and then the real panic would bang in and you'd reach out and try to touch the guy in front of you, groping for his shirt, hoping to Christ he was still there. It made for some bad dreams.

Dave Jensen popped special vitamins high in carotene. Lieutenant Cross popped NoDoz. Henry Dobbins and Norman Bowker even rigged up a safety line between them, a long piece of string tied to their belts. The whole platoon felt the impact.

With Rat Kiley, though, it was different. Too many body bags, maybe. Too much gore.

At first Rat just sank inside himself, not saying a word, but then later on, after five or six days, it flipped the other way. He couldn't stop talking. Weird talk, too. Talking about bugs, for instance: how the worst thing in Nam was the goddamn bugs. Big giant killer bugs, he'd say, mutant bugs, bugs with fucked-up DNA, bugs that were chemically altered by napalm and defoliants and tear gas and DDT. He claimed the bugs were personally after his ass. He said he could hear the bastards homing in on him. Swarms of mutant bugs, billions of them, they had him bracketed. Whispering his name, he said—his actual name— all night long—it was driving him crazy.

Odd stuff, Sanders said, and it wasn't just talk. Rat developed some peculiar habits. Constantly scratching himself. Clawing at the bug bites. He couldn't quit digging at his skin, making big scabs and then ripping off the scabs and scratching the open sores.

It was a sad thing to watch. Definitely not the old Rat Kiley. His whole personality seemed out of kilter.

To an extent, though, everybody was feeling it. The long night marches turned their minds upside down; all the rhythms were wrong. Always a lost sensation. They'd blunder along through the dark, willy-nilly, no sense of place or direction, probing for an enemy that nobody could see. Like a snipe hunt, Sanders said. A bunch of dumb Cub Scouts chasing the phantoms. They'd march north for a time, then east, then north again, skirting the villages, no one talking except in whispers. And it was rugged country, too. Not quite mountains, but rising fast, full of gorges and deep brush and places you could die. Around midnight things always got wild. All around you, everywhere, the whole dark countryside came alive. You'd hear a strange hum in your ears. Nothing specific; nothing you could put a name on. Tree frogs, maybe, or snakes or flying squirrels or who-knew-what. Like the night had its own voice—that hum in your ears—and in the hours after midnight you'd swear you were walking through some kind of soft black protoplasm, Vietnam, the blood and the flesh.

It was no joke, Sanders said. The monkeys chattered deathchatter. The nights got freaky.

Rat Kiley finally hit a wall.

He couldn't sleep during the hot daylight hours; he couldn't cope with the nights.

Late one afternoon, as the platoon prepared for another march, he broke down in front of Mitchell Sanders. Not crying, but up against it. He said he was scared. And it wasn't normal scared. He didn't know *what* it was: too long in-country, probably. Or else he wasn't cut out to be a medic. Always policing up the parts, he said. Always plugging up holes. Sometimes he'd stare at guys who were still okay, the alive guys, and he'd start to picture how they'd look dead. Without arms or legs—that sort of thing. It was ghoulish, he knew that, but he couldn't shut off the pictures. He'd be sitting there talking with Bowker or Dobbins or somebody, just marking time, and then out of nowhere he'd find himself wondering how much the guy's head weighed, like how *heavy* it was, and what it would feel like to pick up the head and carry it over to a chopper and dump it in.

Rat scratched the skin at his elbow, digging in hard. His eyes were red and weary.

"It's not right," he said. "These pictures in my head, they won't quit. I'll see a guy's liver. The actual fucking *liver*. And the thing is, it doesn't scare me, it doesn't even give me the willies. More like curiosity. The way a doctor feels when he looks at a patient, sort of mechanical, not seeing the real person, just a ruptured appendix or a clogged-up artery."

His voice floated away for a second. He looked at Sanders and tried to smile.

He kept clawing at his elbow.

"Anyway," Rat said, "the days aren't so bad, but at night the pictures get to be a bitch. I start seeing my own body. Chunks of myself. My own heart, my own kidneys. It's like—I don't know—it's like staring into this huge black crystal ball. One of these nights I'll be lying dead out there in the dark and nobody'll find me except the bugs—I can *see* it—I can see the goddamn bugs chewing tunnels through me—I can see the mongooses munching on my bones. I swear, it's too much. I can't keep seeing myself dead."

Mitchell Sanders nodded. He didn't know what to say. For a while they sat watching the shadows come, then Rat shook his head.

He said he'd done his best. He'd tried to be a decent medic. Win some and lose some, he said, but he'd tried hard. Briefly then, rambling a little, he talked about a few of the guys who were gone now, Curt Lemon and Kiowa and Ted Lavender, and how crazy it was that people who were so incredibly alive could get so incredibly dead.

Then he almost laughed.

"This whole war," he said. "You know what it is? Just one big banquet. Meat, man. You and me. Everybody. Meat for the bugs."

The next morning he shot himself.

He took off his boots and socks, laid out his medical kit, doped himself up, and put a round through his foot.

Nobody blamed him, Sanders said.

Before the chopper came, there was time for good-byes. Lieutenant Cross went over and said he'd vouch that it was an accident. Henry Dobbins and Azar gave him a stack of comic books for hospital reading. Everybody stood in a little circle, feeling bad about it, trying to cheer him up with bullshit about the great night life in Japan.

THE SOUTH POLAR NIGHT

FREDERICK A. COOK

Frederick Albert Cook (1865–1940) signed on for his first polar expedition shortly after graduating as a doctor from New York University. On his return from the Arctic, he joined a Belgian expedition to Antarctica in 1897. As ship's surgeon, he kept a diary of the physical and psychological impact of two months of darkness, published as *Through the First Antarctic Night* (1900). Cook saved the crew by insisting on a diet of raw meat and by suggesting that an escape canal be sawed through the ice. He survived to journey again to the Arctic, claiming to be the first to reach the North Pole in 1908, a full year before Robert Peary. A vicious controversy ensued, which gave the laurels to Peary, though many now credit Cook with that polar first.

.   .   .

MAY 16. —THE LONG night began at 12 o'clock last night. We did not know this until this afternoon. At 4 o'clock Lecointe got an observation by two stars which placed us in latitude 71° 34′ 30″

longitude 89° 10′. According to a careful calculation from these figures the captain announces the melancholy news that there will be no more day—no more sun for seventy days . . .

The winter and the darkness have slowly but steadily settled over us. By such easy stages has the light departed that we have not, until now, appreciated the awful effect. The circumstance has furnished a subject for our conversation for most of the time which we now mis-name day, and a large part of the sleeping hours of the night. It is not difficult to read on the faces of my companions their thoughts and their moody dispositions. We are all wandering northward—homeward, with the fugitive sun. The curtain of blackness which has fallen over the outer world of icy desolation has also descended upon the inner world of our souls. Around the tables, in the laboratory, and in the forecastle, men are sitting about sad and dejected, lost in dreams of melancholy from which, now and then, one arouses with an empty attempt at enthusiasm. For brief moments some try to break the spell by jokes, told perhaps for the fiftieth time. Others grind out a cheerful philosophy; but all efforts to infuse bright hopes fail . . .

May 17.—At ten o'clock this morning the purple twilight curve settled over the south-west, edged with an indescribable blending of orange, red, and gold, and at eleven o'clock this curve was met by a zone of rose which gradually ascended over the north-east, above the sun. The ice, which had been gray, was lighted up by a lively flash of pink, which was relieved by long river-like leads of open water having a glowing surface of dark violet. These, however, were the surface colours towards the sun. In the opposite direction there was an entirely different effect. The snow had spread evenly over it a delicate shade of green, while the waters were a very dark purple-blue. A few minutes before twelve a great, distorted, ill-defined semi-globular mass of fire rose over the north, edged along the line of sharp hummocks, and then sank beneath the ice. It was an image of the sun, lifted above its actual position by the refractive character of the air, through which its light passed to our eyes. It was in reality an optical illusion, based upon the principle that if a beam of light is compelled to pass through a medium of various densities, as the air here is sure to be, its course is deflected. The sun, then, though actually below the horizon to-day, was raised by this apparent uplift and we were able to see one-half of his face . . .

May 20.—It is the fifth day of the long night and it certainly seems long, very long, since we have felt the heat of the sun . . .

I have selected this part of the day to take a daily walk over the pack to neighbouring floes, and to distant icebergs, to study the ice and the life, and to obtain sufficient physical exercise, as well as mental recreation, to retard the spell of indifference which is falling over me.

For fifteen minutes before and after twelve o'clock the sky and the ice are flooded by a wealth of fascinating colours. The northern sky is such that one momentarily expects the sun to rise. Here are the warm shades of red and yellow and on the snow, looking in this direction, there is a noticeable flesh colour in which one sees fetching lines of lilac. In the opposite direction there are some weird shades of blue-black and a few dead sheets of gray-blue in shadowed surfaces, in the caverns of bergs, and in the fissures, but the mixed shades of green and purple and violet are also displayed with crystal purity. I cannot describe this short spell of mid-day glory as it impresses me. If I could wield a brush, and lay these colours on canvas I feel that one of the ambitions of my life would be accomplished. But I cannot—and what am I to do in black, with an overworked pen, frosty ink, and a mind which is wearied as soon as the cheer of noon-day passes . . .

May 27.—The little dusk at midday is fading more and more. A feeble deflected light falls upon the elevations, the icebergs, and the hummocks, offering a faint cheerfulness, but this soon withdraws and leaves a film of blackness. The pack presents daily the same despondent surface of gray which, by contrast to the white sparkle of some time ago, makes our outlook even more melancholy . . .

Generally we are able to see the stars from two in the afternoon until ten in the morning. During the four hours of midday the sky is generally screened by a thick icy vapour. There are a few white petrels about daily, and in the sounding hole we have noticed a seal occasionally, but there is now no other life. All have an abundance of work, but our ambition for regular occupation, particularly anything which requires prolonged mental concentration, is wanting; even the task of keeping up the log is too much. There is nothing new to write about, nothing to excite fresh interest. There are now no auroras, and no halos; everything on the frozen sea and over it is sleeping the long sleep of the frigid night.

May 28.—The grayness of the first days of the night has given way to a soul-despairing darkness, broken only at noon by a feeble yellow haze on the northern sky. I can think of nothing more disheartening, more destructive to human energy, than this dense, unbroken blackness of the long polar night . . .

May 31.—The regular routine of our work is tiresome in the extreme, not because it is difficult of execution or requires great physical exertion, but because of its monotony. Day after day, week after week, and month after month we rise at the same hour, eat the same things, talk on the same subjects, make a pretense of doing the same work, and look out upon the same icy wilderness. We try hard to introduce new topics for thought and new concoctions for the weary stomach. We strain the truth to introduce stories of home and of flowery future prospects, hoping to infuse a new cheer; but it all fails miserably. We are under the spell of the black antarctic night, and, like the world which it darkens, we are cold, cheerless, and inactive. We have aged ten years in thirty days . . .

June 1.—It is now difficult to get out of our warm beds in the morning. There is no dawn—nothing to mark the usual division of night and morning until nearly noon. During the early part of the night it is next to impossible to go to sleep, and if we drink coffee we do not sleep at all. When we do sink into a slumber, it is so deep that we are not easily awakened. Our appetites are growing smaller and smaller, and the little food which is consumed gives much trouble. Oh, for that heavenly ball of fire! Not for the heat—the human economy can regulate that—but for the light—the hope of life . . .

June 4.—The ice is again breaking and the pressure of the floes, as they ride over each other, makes a noise converting the otherwise dark quietude into a howling scene of groans. It is again snowing . . .

June 19.—It is dark! dark! Dark at noon, dark at midnight, dark every hour of the day. And thus we jog along day after day, through the unbroken sameness. There is plenty of work close at hand. The weather should be carefully studied; the sky and the frozen sea contain problems for solution. We are in a world unknown, but just at present we care little about our novel position or our future rewards.

The darkness grows daily a little deeper, and the night soaks hourly a little more colour from our blood. Our gait is now careless, the step non-elastic, the foothold uncertain. The hair grows quickly, like plants in a hot-house, but there is a great change in the colour. Most of us in the cabin have grown decidedly gray within two months, though few are over thirty. Our faces are drawn, and there is an absence of jest and cheer and hope in our make-up which, in itself, is one of the saddest incidents in our existence. There is no one willing to openly confess the force of the night upon himself, but the novelty of life has been worn out and the cold, dark outside world is incapable of introducing anything new. The moonlight comes and goes alike, during the hours of midday as at midnight. The stars glisten over the gloomy snows . . .

June 22.—It is midnight and midwinter. Thirty-five long, dayless nights have passed. An equal number of dreary, cheerless days must elapse before we again see the glowing orb, the star of day. The sun has reached its greatest northern declination. We have thus passed the antarctic midnight. The winter solstice is to us the meridian day, the zenith of the night as much so as twelve o'clock is the meridian hour to those who dwell in the more favoured lands, in the temperate and tropical zones, where there is a regular day and night three hundred and sixty-five times in the yearly cycle. Yesterday was the darkest day of the night; a more dismal sky and a more depressing scene could not be imagined, but to-day the outlook is a little brighter. The sky is lined with a few touches of orange, the frozen sea of black snow is made more cheerful by the high lights, with a sort of dull phospherescent glimmer of the projecting peaks of ice . . .

June 29.—Since my last writing there has been nothing to mark time or disturb the gloom of the long black monotony . . .

July 12.—The light is daily increasing at midday, which should be a potent encouragement, but we are failing in fortitude and in physical force. From day to day we all complain of a general enfeeblement of strength, of insufficient heart action, of a mental lethargy, and of a universal feeling of discomfort . . .

July 14.—Almost everybody is alarmed and coming to me for medical treatment, for real or imaginary troubles. The complaints differ considerably, but the underlying cause is the same in all. We are developing a form of anaemia peculiar to the polar regions. An anaemia which I had noticed before among the members of the first Peary Arctic Expedition, but our conditions are much more serious . . .

July 15.—The weather continues cold, but clear and calm, the only three qualities which make the antarctic climate endurable during the night. There is now much light. One can read ordinary print at 9 AM, and at noon the north is flushed with a glory of green and orange and yellow. We are still very feeble. An exercise of one hour sends the pulse up to 130, but we have all learned to like and crave penguin meat. To sleep is our most difficult task, and to avoid work is the mission of everybody. Arctowski says, "We are in a mad-house," and our humour points that way.

July 17.—If we had not fresh meat to eat and an abundance of fuel to give heat, I am sure we would have an alarming mortality in less than a month. Several lives have certainly been saved by eating penguins, and we shall always owe them a debt of gratitude. And now the sun though invisible is rising higher and higher under the horizon, giving us a long dawn from nine until three o'clock. Everybody is advancing in cheerfulness with the rising sun, but physically we are in a deplorable condition. Alcohol, even in small quantities, has now a deleterious effect upon us. We have been accustomed to take light wines at meals, but the wine has a bad effect upon the heart and kidney functions, so much so that we have stopped its use altogether.

July 19.—The northern sky gives every promise of soon sending forth the sun. The shades of dawn are first green, then orange-red, followed by a bright yellow, so bright that one almost imagines a sight of the upper rim of the sun. The ice for days has been intensely purple . . .

July 21.—The night is clear and sharp, with a brightness in the sky and a blueness on the ice which we have not seen since the first few days after sunset. An aurora of unusual brightness is arched across the southern sky. The transformation in its figure is rapid, and the wavy movement is strikingly noticeable. We are all out looking at the aurora, some by way of curiosity, but others are seriously studying the phenomenon . . .

July 22.—After so much physical, mental, and moral depression, and after having our anticipations raised to a fever heat by the tempting increase of dawn at noon, it is needless to say that we are elated at the expectation of actual daylight once more. In these dreadful wastes of perennial ice and snow, man feels the force of the superstitions of past ages, and becomes willingly a worshipper of the eternal luminary. I am certain that if our preparations for greeting the returning sun were seen by other people, either civilised or savage, we would be thought disciples of heliolatry.

Every man on board has long since chosen a favourite elevation from which to watch the coming sight. Some are in the crow's nest, others on the ropes and spars of the rigging; but these are the men who do little travelling. The adventurous fellows are scattered over the pack upon icebergs and high hummocks. These positions were taken at about eleven o'clock. The northern sky at this time was nearly clear and clothed with the usual haze. A bright lemon glow was just changing into an even glimmer of rose. At about half-past eleven a few stratus clouds spread over the rose, and under these there was a play in colours, too complex for my powers of description. The clouds were at first violet, but they quickly caught the train of colours which was spread over the sky beyond. There were spaces of gold, orange, blue, green, and a hundred harmonious blends, with an occasional strip like a band of polished silver to set the colours in bold relief. Precisely at twelve o'clock a fiery cloud separated, disclosing a bit of the upper rim of the sun . . .

For several minutes my companions did not speak. Indeed, we could not at that time have found words with which to express the buoyant feeling of relief, and the emotion of the new life which was sent coursing through our arteries by the hammer-like beats of our enfeebled hearts.

DARKNESS VISIBLE

GRETEL EHRLICH

G̲retel Ehrlich (1946–) trained as a filmmaker but turned early to writing, publishing two collections of poetry before her debut book of essays, *The Solace of Open Spaces* (1984). This was followed by a collection of short fiction, *Drinking the Dry Clouds* (1985), a novel, *Heart Mountain* (1987), and a second essay collection, *Islands, the Universe, Home* (1991). Injured by lightning on her Wyoming ranch, Ehrlich documented her recovery in *A Match to the Heart* (1994). That same year she began travelling to Greenland, obsessed by a landscape and culture shaped by ice. *This Cold Heaven: Seven Seasons in Greenland* (2002), excerpted here, is part travelogue, part cultural anthropology. "It's like being in a dark theater," Ehrlich says of the Arctic night. "Your imagination works in different and alarming ways."

. . .

MORNING. I'M NOT living on earth or ice but rock and the sharp tooth of Uummannaq Mountain jutting up behind the town like a harpoon. At eleven the peak caught light like the poisoned tip of an arrow and the cliffs that gave birth to the moon last night were pink, crimson, and gold. By noon, there was a bit of light in the sky, but not enough to read by.

At two AM, against the dogs' constant conversation about urgent matters of food, sex, and rank and their general angst at being chained on dirty patches of rock and snow and not being fed enough, I lay alone. The moon was down. Unable to sleep, I drank a cheap bottle of blanc de noirs—the white of the black, the foam of the night, the light hidden within dark grapes and made to sparkle. But how did they get white from black, how did they separate the two?

It no longer mattered whether I closed my eyes. The operations of the mind were the same: darkness made being awake seem dreamlike. I wondered how it would be to live in a house made of ice, and thought of the way light filtered through shoji screens. Japanese culture, like that of the Eskimos, evolved in relative darkness without electric light. Racially linked, both cultures might have produced the same theater: in No plays, the whitefaced actor was meant to be the only light on the stage, teeth blackened as if to simplify human physiology to a ghost acquainted with death or to toothless infancy. Up here, an Eskimo's moon face grew darker and darker the more months he lived out on the ice; in the all-light spring months, his face was a negative image of the sun.

When all the blanc was gone there was only noir, *obscurum per obscuris,* a path leading nowhere, or maybe to the town dump.

The Inuit never made much of beginnings or endings and now I knew why. No matter what you did in winter, how deep you dove, there was still no daylight and no comprehension that came with light. Endings were everywhere, visible within the invisible, and the timeless days and nights ticked by.

Greenlanders say that only the *qanuallit*—the white people—are afraid of the dark, while Eskimos like nothing better than long winter days of storytelling and talking to spirits. Rasmussen told the story of two Danes—Gustav and Olaf—who overwintered together every year on the east coast of Greenland, where they hunted foxes and sold the skins in the spring. Olaf made dinner one night. Later, Gustav said he had a bad stomachache. Shortly after, he died sitting in his chair. In Olaf's grief and the shock of utter solitude, he found he could not part with his friend. He set Gustav's corpse, still in the chair, outside to freeze and in the evenings brought him back inside, seating him at the dinner table so he would not have to eat alone. In the spring, when Gustav began to thaw, Olaf took him home to Denmark to be buried.

In my frigid room I read about dark nebulae—immense clouds composed of the detritus of dying stars. The nebulae are made of molecular hydrogen, high concentrations of gas and dust whose effect in the universe is to produce "visual extinction." Yet the nebulae are detectable because of the obscuration they cause. I looked up at the sky: the dark patches between constellations are not blanks but dense interstellar clouds through which light from distant stars cannot pass. They are known variously as the Snake, the Horsehead, the Coalsack. Darkness is not a blank, a negation, but a rich and dense obstruction, a kind of cosmic chocolate, a forest of stellar events whose presences are only known by their invisibility.

A skin of ice formed, smoothing watery wrinkles to glass. Somewhere out in the darkness I heard the rhythmic drone of a ship's diesel engine, then a sound like sheet metal collapsing: it was the ship breaking a path through the ice. Inside the harbor, the captain turned the ship around and backed to the dock. He would have to break ice with the bow to leave again.

When the harbor was quiet again and the crew had walked home, ice began to congeal around the ship's bow. One deck-light was left on. In its hard, downward beam I saw that snow had begun to fall. When I looked again, the ship's deck had turned white.

IN WINTER, light sources are reversed. Snow-covered earth is a torch and the sky is a blotter that soaks up everything visible. There is no sun, but the moon lives on borrowed time and borrowed light. Home late from hunting, two men pulled a sledge up a hill laden with freshly killed seals, dripping a trail of blood in the snow. As I dozed off, I dreamed the paths were all red and the sky was ice and the water was coal. I took a handful of water and drew with it: in a frozen sky, I drew a black sun.

Later I couldn't sleep. The half-moon's slow rising seemed like a form of exhaustion, with night trying to hold the moon's head under water. It bobbed up anyway, and I, its captive audience, caught the illuminated glacial cliffs on the surface of my eyes. The moon's light was reflected light, but from what source? The sun was a flood that blinded us, a sun we couldn't see. When I lay back in the dark, the pupils of my eyes opened.

At birth, one group of Eskimos held the newly expelled placenta in front of a chosen infant's face as if it were a piece of glass. From it came light and the ability to see inward. I looked out my window: it returned my reflection. Beyond, I saw nothing.

Once Rasmussen asked a shaman, "What do you think of the way men live?" The shaman answered, "They live brokenly, mingling all things together; weakly, because they cannot do one thing at a time."

I tried to do less and less every day, tried weeding out the mind. To obtain awareness was once thought by the Inuit to be an essential aspect of personhood. The confines of village life meant that behavior had to be moderate. Even-temperedness, humor, and modesty were highly valued; cautionary tales warned people about the harm anger and self-pity could cause. Once, a woman who had been wronged by her husband became so distraught that she flew on a bearskin to find him, and when she did, she mutilated him until he was dead. After, the bearskin sewed itself to the front of her body and she was never able to get it off again.

Seeing was the ultimate act of the angakoks. Whether it was seeing into the source of a famine or the source of an illness, they had to pierce all obstacles. In eastern Greenland, and in Alaska, some shamans and their apprentices wore masks. Others hid their faces behind sealskins. In both cases, the idea was to banish the obstructions of ego, greed, contempt, or self-importance that might get in the way. The neutrality of the face-cover provided a passageway to another world.

To believe that the single soul was made up of many strands of beings was normal. What else could be expected from a people who lived in total darkness for three months of the year and spent their lives driving dogsleds over ice that concealed the very thing they needed to see in order to survive?

The Inuit scratched their imaginations against their frozen world as if it were a flint: light came into their bodies, enabling them to see, to pierce ice, to fly under water, or go to the moon. Once when a European explorer arrived at a camp and set up a telescope, the hunters laughed at him; their shamans could already go to the moon or the stars without help.

THREE 'ANTE MERIDIEM'

DONALD CULROSS PEATTIE

Trained as a botanist, Donald Culross Peattie (1898–1964) began writing as a nature columnist for the *Washington Star* in 1924, eventually publishing almost forty books of travel, children's, and nature literature. A man trained in both the sciences and the arts (he studied French poetry before switching to botany), Peattie is most famed for two comprehensive guides to trees published in the fifties, later combined, abridged, and reissued as *A Natural History of North American Trees* in 2007. He moved to rural Illinois during the Depression and produced two books in archaic literary forms: *An Almanac for Moderns* (1935) and *A Book of Hours* (1937), the source of this selection. As he moves through the hours of the night, Peattie contemplates a time in the diurnal cycle that is lost, for the most part, to even the most observant among us.

. . .

ON SLEEP'S FRINGE there is a tremulous, mirage-like realm, a long, narrow kingdom like Egypt's land, with the shape of a scythe and the feel of a sea strand. It is neither the ocean of oblivion, nor the continent of waking. Here the small waves whisper and flash; the half-drowned swimmer lies beached, innocently, with his face in the warmth of sand, and the ebb of sleep lapping his tranquil nakedness. He knows that life is given him back, but is not sure yet that he does not regret the sweetness of death. He hears the insistent whistle of some unknown land bird, who praises the reality to which he will not yet open his lids. He is glad of the bird, and the land, but he clings to the marginal sands of this slender realm.

That realm is neither of Ra nor of Dis. And the hour is not the butterfly's nor the moth's. It is crepuscular, but of the two twilights in the rhythm of planetary rotation it is the more mysterious. Should the dreamer fully awake to the dawn twilight, he would find himself still in a watery half-world, where bats and nighthawks flit. And they say that the great cecropia, the mysterious soft giant of all his tribe, alone of them takes wing in the hour before sunrise. But do fireflies dance again, that quench their light after midnight? Do the vesper sparrows, suddenly, after the night silence, speak again into the thin dark? The midges and mosquitoes, do they hold a second dervish rout, and are there swallows to sweep after them now as at dusk?

The dreamer does not focus his thoughts on the neglected Nature of dawn twilight. Precision is a beam that will pierce through this precious opalescent light. Only to the calling of the bird, the sweet, reiterant whistle without a name, will he open his ears while the waves lap him. One thing at a time, says the soul, one thing, and very slowly.

For this is the moment when the creative power, the indefinable, uncomprehended imagination, works clay with its lover's fingers. It makes its own dreams; it accepts the sea-wrack forms, the shell-money of Poseidon, the spawn of the subconscious, and, itself alert as never in the waking hours, it weighs each coin, hoarding the precious, shoving dross away.

Imagination knows no limits; it has no shames, and is not even civilized; it is not conscious of itself, calls itself by no names. Just so, the dreamer forgets that he is a man, with a name, with a profession, a certain number of years to his life, a known number in the past, an unknown remainder left to him. He is like a child, yet not a child, for in this hour, lying on that shingle that is his bed, a man has none of a child's bird-like extraversion, nor its rapid avian pulse, nor the power to sleep—dead but warm-dead.

In this hour the faculty called poetry (vaguely enough but perhaps truly) performs its services for the day. Poetry is not the whole of artistic creation, even for a worker in words. Information, organization, even the most finished or appealing styles, and matters of craft that only the cleared awakened mind can master. To have something to say, one must endure, one must receive the actual impact of experience upon the senses. Field experience, the naturalists would call it. Brushes with other humans, peeps into books, the passing landscape of the world we move in—these are diurnal realities. They may suffice for very competent creation. But they are not the stuff of imagination.

Whether imagination is a useful or even a safe commodity

has been questioned from the beginning of time, and may be doubted to the end. There have been unfortunate men who have so loved or so needed it that, to prolong or to regain the lost twilight strand, they have given their days to chloral, or fled to the last desperate jungle sanctuary of madness. But for the sane the narrow kingdom is sweet. One may not stay long there. The calling of the bird begins to trouble, and the outgoing tide sucks the sand from under the feet. You have to choose between the bird and the depths, and the soul in health will always turn to the light.

The bidden consciousness uprises. The part of the mind that analyses and identifies now names the bird. It is the whip-poor-will, a creature of the very hour, a singer who gives two performances in the cycle, the one in the evening well attended, and the other to a wood where there are few auditors. The dawn song lacks full confidence; it is only a salutation, a recognition of the dusk that dies in light instead of darkness. Already, as the wakening man identifies it, the bird has ceased to trust its own voice. With a few soft last cries it ends its orisons.

ACKNOWLEDGMENTS

"The Raven Steals the Light" excerpted from *The Raven Steals the Light* by Bill Reid and Robert Bringhurst. (Vancouver: Douglas & McIntyre, 1984.)

"First Night" excerpted from *Acquainted With the Night: Excursions Through the World After Dark* by Christopher Dewdney. Copyright © 2004 by Christopher Dewdney. Published by HarperCollins Publishers Ltd. With permission of the author. All rights reserved.

"Shadow World" excerpted from *A Natural History of the Senses* by Diane Ackerman. Copyright © 1990 by Diane Ackerman. Used by permission of Random House, Inc.

"Navigating the Nightscape" excerpted from *At Day's Close: Night in Times Past* by A. Roger Ekirch. Copyright © 2005 by A. Roger Ekirch. Used by permission of W.W. Norton & Company, Inc.

"Beginnings" excerpted from *Seeing in the Dark* by Timothy Ferris. Copyright © 2002 by Timothy Ferris. Reprinted with permission of Simon & Schuster, Inc. All rights reserved.

"Total Eclipse," pp. 87–93, excerpted from *Teaching a Stone to Talk: Expeditions and Encounters* by Annie Dillard. Copright © 1982 by Annie Dillard. Reprinted by permission of HarperCollins Publishers.

"De Stella Nova" excerpted from "On a New Star" by Tycho Brahe, in *A Source Book in Astronomy* by Harlow Shapley and Helen Howarth, eds. (New York: McGraw-Hill, 1929.)

"The Shape of Night" excerpted from *The Soul of the Night: An Astronomical Pilgrimage* by Chet Raymo. (New Jersey: Prentice-Hall, 1985.)

"The Moonwatchers of Lascaux" excerpted from *The Moon: A Biography* by David Whitehouse. (London: Headline Book Publishing, 2001.)

"Nocturne" excerpted from *Bringing Back the Dodo: Lessons in Natural and Unnatural History* by Wayne Grady © 2006. Published by McClelland & Stewart Ltd. Used with permission of the publisher.

"Night Fishing" reproduced from *Fishless Days, Angling Nights* with the permission of the Estate of Alfred W. Miller.

"The Alligators of Lake Dexter" excerpted from *Travels through North & South Carolina, Georgia, East & West Florida, the Cherokee Country, the Extensive Territories of the Muscogulges, or Creek Confederacy, and the Country of the Chactaws* by William Bartram. (Philadelphia: James & Johnson, 1791.)

"Night on the Great Beach" excerpted from *The Outermost House: A Year of Life on the Great Beach of Cape Cod* by Henry Beston. Copyright © 1928,

"In the Dark" excerpted from *Sun After Dark: Flights into the Foreign* by Pico Iyer. Copyright © 2004 by Pico Iyer. Used by permission of Alfred A. Knopf, a division of Random House, Inc.

"Night Life" excerpted from *The Things They Carried* by Tim O'Brien. Copyright © 1990 by Tim O'Brien. Reprinted by permission of Houghton Mifflin Harcourt Publishing Company. All rights reserved.

"The South Polar Night" excerpted from *Through the First Antarctic Night 1898–1899* by Frederick. A. Cook. (Montreal: McGill-Queen's University Press, 1980.)

"Darkness Visible" excerpted from *This Cold Heaven* by Gretel Ehrlich. (London: Fourth Estate, 2002.)

"Three *Ante Meridiem*" excerpted from *A Book of Hours* by Donald Culross Peattie. (London: George G. Harrap & Co. Ltd., 1938.)

The David Suzuki Foundation works through science and education to protect the diversity of nature and our quality of life, now and for the future.

With a goal of achieving sustainability within a generation, the Foundation collaborates with scientists, business and industry, academia, government and non-governmental organizations. We seek the best research to provide innovative solutions that will help build a clean, competitive economy that does not threaten the natural services that support all life.

The Foundation is a federally registered independent charity, which is supported with the help of over 50,000 individual donors across Canada and around the world.

We invite you to become a member. For more information on how you can support our work, please contact us:

The David Suzuki Foundation
219–2211 West 4th Avenue
Vancouver, BC
Canada V6K 4S2
www.davidsuzuki.org
contact@davidsuzuki.org
Tel: 604-732-4228 · Fax: 604-732-0752

Checks can be made payable to The David Suzuki Foundation.
All donations are tax-deductible.
Canadian charitable registration: (BN) 12775 6716 RR0001
U.S. charitable registration: #94-3204049